Praise f...

Ariel Garfinkel powerfully remin... Vietnam is not over for the Vietnamese. In spite o... ho work ...o ensure that we comply with international law and treaty obligations, the U.S. has failed to acknowledge and fully fund our responsibility to clean up the munitions and chemicals left behind in Vietnam. And the cost of that cavalier attitude is that more Vietnamese have died or been maimed from our weapons since we withdrew military forces than the number of Americans who died in the entire war. While these continuing deaths could have been avoided, the damage to the environment and future generations from chemicals cannot be avoided now, but with adequate funding could be mitigated. Until we Americans act on this knowledge and face our responsibility the war cannot be over for us either.

— AMBASSADOR SAM BROWN

U.S. Representative, Conference on Security and Cooperation in Europe; Coordinator, Vietnam Moratorium Committee

The US wars in Indochina are among the most severe crimes of post-World War II history, crimes compounded by the unwillingness of the perpetrators to recognize what they have done and to try to compensate in some manner for the terrible human consequences. As Ariel Garfinkel demonstrates in this revealing study, the crimes persist to the presen... ...el and fundamental issues of internatior... ...ave yet to be confronted, a matte... ...ure exercises of state power.

JOAM CHOMSKY
...eritus, M.I.T.

After the devastating Vietnam War, the U.S. government left behind people and lands poisoned by Agent Orange/dioxin. Descendants of those exposed to these deadly chemicals continue to suffer serious diseases and horrific birth defects. This important book details why the U.S. refusal to compensate the victims of its chemical warfare violates international law.

— MARJORIE COHN
Co-Coordinator, Vietnam Agent Orange Relief Campaign
Professor Emerita, Thomas Jefferson School of Law

For Vietnam, the wartime suffering has never ended. Nor has America's refusal to acknowledge its responsibility for causing that continued suffering or to fulfill its legal obligations to alleviate it. Ariel Garfinkel illuminates both of these failures by our country, and calls on us to rise at last to these challenges. It is long past due—but never too late—for us to heed her call.

— DANIEL ELLSBERG
Author, *The Doomsday Machine* and
Secrets: A Memoir of Vietnam and the Pentagon Papers

Ariel Garfinkel's book shows why the war is not yet over for the Vietnamese, and she brilliantly lays out the ongoing ravages of Agent Orange and unexploded ordnance. Scofflaw is a detailed accounting of how, more than 50 years after the 'end' of the war, the U.S. has failed to take responsibility for the continuing casualties.

— JEAN GRASSMAN
Associate Professor, CUNY Graduate School of
Public Health and Policy

For decades the U.S. has claimed it has no legal obligation to address the impact of its weapons that continue to injure and kill tens of thousands in Vietnam, Laos and Cambodia. Ms. Garfinkel makes a clear case that the U.S. government can no longer hide behind the argument that its weapons were legal at the time. At the very least it has a moral and humanitarian duty to address the continuing impact now that the prohibition of these weapons has become the international norm. Scofflaw will be useful for those advocating for the U.S. to do more to address war legacies in Southeast Asia, including the environmental and human impacts of weapons used in more recent years.

— SUSAN HAMMOND

Founder and Director, War Legacies Project

Ariel Garfinkel provides a brisk introduction to the residual humanitarian issues remaining in Vietnam, even in 2017, from the war that ended nearly fifty years ago. There remains a compelling case for the U.S. to see through the removal of the landmines and unexploded ordnance, and to clean up dioxin contaminated locations in Vietnam ... and, I believe, to provide modest assistance to the families proximate to Agent Orange contamination whose genetically deformed children they struggle to raise.

— DAVID HAWK

Former Cambodia Director
Office of the U.N. High Commissioner for Human Rights

Promising new energy is added to the international human rights movement by this work of the young scholar Ariel Garfinkel of Columbia University. In her penetrating analysis of U.S. failure to comply with international law when leaving Vietnam (resulting in the continuing deaths of innocent villagers who step on unexploded American bombs even today), Garfinkel poignantly identifies the biggest challenge in promoting human rights around the world— making sure that the UN Declaration of Human Rights and other relevant treaty laws have real teeth instead of being platitudes ignored at the whim of powerful states. This is her goal and hopefully that of a new generation of scholar-activists.

— JOHN G. "JACK" HEALEY

Executive Director, Amnesty International USA (1982-1994)

The careful scholarship reflected in Scofflaw *is truly remarkable. While it took years for our government to acknowledge that American soldiers were severely harmed by Agent Orange exposure in Vietnam, it has never admitted that spraying this toxic substance across Vietnam also harmed its innocent civilians—and continues to cause severe birth deformities to this day. Taking ownership of the devastation we caused in Vietnam and aiding victims who continue to suffer as a result should be a priority.*

— HON. BARBARA LEE

United States Congress

This penetrating analysis by a remarkable young scholar should give pause to all policymakers about the role of war on the world stage. It also is a wake-up call for the U.S. and other nations about the vital importance of our adherence to international law.

— **HON. JOHN LEWIS**
United States Congress

If you think the war in Vietnam ended in 1975, you need to read this book. It's a powerful statement about our moral and legal obligations to clean up the unexploded ordnance, landmines and chemical toxins that continue to harm innocent people in that country.

— **BOBBY MULLER**
Founder, Vietnam Veterans of America
Co-founder, International Campaign to Ban Landmines
(1997 Nobel Peace Prize)

Ms. Garfinkel's book explores the great tragedy of Agent Orange use in Vietnam and its deep lingering consequences for a generation born after the war was over. She makes a very serious contribution to the scholarly debate about international law, its limitations, its jurisdiction and how it plays a part in pushing political discussion. Scofflaw also lets the reader understand how Senator Pat Leahy of Vermont moved the United States to take responsibility and to provide a pathway for more remediation.

— **LYNN NOVICK**
Producer, Florentine Films (Co-producer of "Vietnam" with Ken Burns)

Over recent decades, Vietnam veterans and many others have felt that a great injustice occurred during and after the war in Viet Nam with America's use of Agent Orange, and our massive bombing campaigns over civilian areas in both the south and the north. The resulting legacy of destruction and loss, pain and suffering— especially the effects of Agent Orange—has affected American veterans and their children, and millions of Vietnamese born after the war. Many have felt a vague discomfort and sadness about this, and others a sense of moral outrage. Some have condemned America for our refusal to be held accountable under accepted standards of human rights and international law—judicial tenets that most of us have not read or researched.

Now Ariel Garfinkel has made it easy. She has compiled into one easy to read book the relevant international laws and protocols which provides compelling evidence of what many citizens of the world have long suspected: that the U.S. has been in violation of some of the most fundamental international laws in our use of Agent Orange and also our massive bombing attacks in Viet Nam. Garfinkel's conclusion, after presenting concrete evidence carefully researched, is that the U.S. is a scofflaw.

As Americans, we are not easily shamed; we rarely admit to error, and never to violations of international law. After reading this book, however, American citizens may wonder how we have escaped, all these years, not just the condemnation of other nations, but international accountability for inhumane and illegal actions which have long been fundamental to global standards of justice.

— CHUCK SEARCY

U.S. Army Military Intelligence (1966-1969)
International Advisor, Project RENEW
Veterans for Peace, Chapter 160

Ariel Garfinkel has written an exhaustive and compelling analysis of the extensive use of conventional weapons and military herbicides during the Vietnam War, and of their continuing presence as a lingering hazard to the Vietnamese people. The data she presents on the sheer magnitude of the problem are eye popping. This book is a compact guide to the complexities of international law and science that are still to be resolved nearly a half century later, with regard to the massive bombing and spraying of Vietnam. With so many persistent unanswered questions, it is heartening that capable young scholars like Garfinkel are still focusing on these issues.

— JEANNE MAGER STELLMAN

Professor Emerita, Mailman School of Public Health, Columbia University

Ariel Garfinkel's impressive analysis weaves together U.S. legacies of war in Vietnam with precise readings of international law. She makes a persuasive case that treaties and conventions do apply retroactively to the unexploded bombs and remaining wartime chemicals in Vietnam, and that U.S. efforts to remediate the damages caused to the Vietnamese people have been far less that what international law requires. Scofflaw should be required reading for the next generation of foreign policy and security specialists who can reverse this disregard for legal norms.

— ANDREW WELLS-DANG

Senior Governance Advisor, Oxfam in Vietnam
Board of Directors, War Legacies Project

Ariel Garfinkel ... reports the facts, awful facts about a war that did not change a grand strategic thing but continues to kill and maim innocent people nevertheless. This book flies in the face of five millennia of human history, doing so with eloquence, copious example and the rule of law.

— COL. LAWRENCE WILKERSON

Former Chief of Staff to U.S. Secretary of State Colin Powell
Visiting Professor of Government, College of William and Mary

SCOFFLAW

SCOFFLAW

International Law and America's Deadly Weapons in Vietnam

Ariel S. Garfinkel

LUCITA
PUBLISHING

Published in the United States by
LUCITÀ Publishing, an imprint of LUCITÀ Inc.
Sunnyvale, California
http://publishing.lucita.net

ISBN-13: 978-19382840-7-6

First LUCITÀ Publishing edition 2018.
LUCITÀ and the sun logo are trademarks of LUCITÀ, Inc.

Cover design by Luba Rasine-Ortoleva
Interior book layout by Scott Keeney

The cover photograph is a public domain image from the United States Agency for International Development (USAID).

Visit www.scofflawbook.com for more information about Scofflaw and Ariel S. Garfinkel.

Publisher's Cataloging-in-Publication Data

Names: Garfinkel, Ariel S., author.
Title: Scofflaw : international law and America's deadly weapons in Vietnam / Ariel S. Garfinkel.
Description: Includes bibliographical references | Sunnyvale, CA: LUCITÀ Publishing, 2018.
Identifiers: ISBN 978-19382840-7-6
Subjects: LCSH Vietnam War, 1961-1975—Equipment and supplies. | Vietnam—Armed Forces—Weapons systems—History—20th century. | United States—Armed Forces—Weapons systems—History—20th century. | Vietnam War, 1961-1975—United States. | War (International law) | International law—United States. | Vietnam War, 1961-1975—Law and legislation—United States. | Military law—United States. | Vietnam War, 1961-1975—Atrocities. | BISAC HISTORY / Military / Vietnam War | POLITICAL SCIENCE / International Relations / Arms Control | LAW / International
Classification: LCC KZ6795 .G37 2018 | DDC 341.6—dc23

Printed in the United States of America on FSC-certified, 30% post consumer recycled paper.

I present this book in honor of all who served in the Vietnam War,
those who gave their lives and those who survived,
American and Vietnamese,
all of them young and all of them wounded

Contents

SCOFFLAW

Acknowledgments

As the adage goes, it truly takes a village. I am grateful to the faculty and staff at Columbia University's Institute for the Study of Human Rights for a superb academic program. I extend special gratitude to my international law advisor and mentor, Professor Belinda Cooper, for teaching me that jurisprudence, like life itself, exists in the grays.

I also benefitted from the unparalleled hospitality of Vietnamese families and public servants who welcomed me with open arms and warm bowls of *pho* during my field research in 2016, including Project RENEW, Vietnam Association for Victims of Agent Orange, and Vietnamese Women's Union. I also am indebted to the scholarly community including Dr. Jeanne Stellman, Dr. Arnold Schecter, Charles Bailey, and the

Hatfield Group, among others whose research exposed the magnitude of ongoing health consequences from the War. As for our veterans, I am most grateful to have learned of their experiences and insights. I give special recognition to Chuck Searcy and Manus Campbell, two veterans who have returned to Vietnam to help its people grapple with the lasting impact of the War.

To the excellent team at LUCITÀ Publishing, many thanks for their terrific work and unwavering support in producing this book. I express special appreciation to Birgitte Rasine for such thorough editing, to Luba Rasine-Ortoleva for her remarkable artistic eye, and to Scott Keeney and the production team for their hard work.

I am particularly grateful to my parents, J. Larry Brown and Judi M. Garfinkel, for their unconditional support even while living across continents. They are the ones who sparked my desire to pursue a career in human rights in the first place.

I salute my colleagues in the field of human rights, known and unknown, whose work is never-ending. In the words of Audre Lorde, *revolution is not a one-time event*. Here's to the revolutions already experienced and those which await us.

Foreword

At a time when Ken Burns and Lynn Novick's eighteen-hour documentary, The Vietnam War, is playing on millions of American televisions—an estimated 400,000 people in Vietnam have seen it as well—and garnering critical comment both positive and negative, this is an extraordinarily relevant book. I attended recently the showing of the documentary's final episode in Washington, DC. Mr. Burns and Ms. Novick introduced the episode and took questions afterward and I must say I was still, several days later, not exactly certain how I felt. My consternation began before the film even rolled, as I read the words emblazoned in red at the top of the introductory title screen: "In war there is no single truth." Inside my head a voice was almost screaming a counterpoint: the Vietnam War has a single truth that explodes all the others no matter how superbly and cinematically portrayed and it is that the war was wrong, devastatingly so. This book's trenchant focus on post-war Vietnam demonstrates part of that wrong.

As a soldier, I fought in Vietnam in 1969 and 1970. At the time, I was as patriotic as any other red-blooded American and felt it my duty to follow the path trod by both my father and father-in-law more than two decades before me, in the Second World War. As a newly-minted soldier in 1966, I got goosebumps when the National Anthem was played and I saluted smartly. At the same time, however, I was a person who would have grudgingly accepted and perhaps even secretly admired the courage of, for example, those NFL football players who have recently displayed their solidarity with the cause of Black Americans by taking a knee during the playing of that anthem. Today, having read Frederick Douglass and studied Black American history at the feet of Colin Powell, I can readily empathize with those players.

The war in Vietnam started me on the process of merging these two very human tendencies—to be a patriot in the conventional sense but to appreciate, even admire, those individuals who powerfully objected—as I know it did for many others. The war began my awakening, slowly, incrementally, but certainly. Some three decades later, when I had finished four years as a U.S. diplomat during much of which I was Chief of Staff to the U.S. Secretary of State, the merger was complete and I knew the truth of both the Second Iraq War and the Vietnam War. They were wrong, and I knew also that dissent in such cases of wrong can be the very highest form of patriotism, particularly if it reveals the often very horrid crimes that lie beneath the American myth. For me, the fact that my country tortured other human beings from 2002–2006 was the ultimate proof. In retrospect, perhaps the Vietnam War should have been.

This book explores the war's tragic legacy. The Burns and Novick film seems mostly—but not entirely—to ignore that legacy in favor of simply adjusting and tweaking the myth a bit. The filmmakers want us, ultimately, to feel angst about the war but more or less conventionally patriotic angst. This book by Ariel Garfinkel, on the other hand, just reports the facts, awful facts about a war that did not change a grand strategic thing but continues to kill and maim innocent people nevertheless. And it continues the injury and killing as the official side of America largely looks the other way. Indeed, that official side has been waging other wars for more than sixteen years now, wars creating their own after-effects, and there is no end in sight and no indication that Washington will act any different after these conflicts end.

On a much wider and even sadder basis than that of simply helping to debunk the American myth about the Vietnam War and about war in general, this book flies in the face of five millennia of human history. That it does so with eloquence, copious example, and the rule of law to buttress it is commendable but not sufficient. The fact that international

law—and the way most of us think about human rights—
supports Ms. Garfinkel's main points about state responsibility
in no way ensures the effective assumption of that responsibility.
From Thucydides' pronouncement on power and the powerful,
to Vice President Dick Cheney's resort to torture and secret
prisons, there is an unbroken line of brutality and cruelty in
the name of monarchy, church and state. And that line parallels
the line of power, as Thucydides tells us—the powerful do what
they will and the powerless have it done to them. Yet I am
reminded of what Sir Nigel Rodley said to me in Siracusa,
Sicily several years ago as we discussed human rights and
international criminal justice (ICJ). I had asked Sir Nigel if the
plethora of human rights and ICJ groups and organizations was
having any real impact. The former UN Special Rapporteur
on Torture replied, with a wry smile: "The more the merrier in
terms of nuisance value."

This book has more than nuisance value, to be sure, as the
raw truth often does. But I fear this book will not be read by
those world leaders most in need of its counsel. Indeed, the
present leader of the world's arguably most powerful country
would likely scoff at it. The man who tweets about nuclear
annihilation of another state would not abide an abridgement
of his power by something as frivolous as thoughts on human
rights or the upholding of international law. Sad to say, a small
minority of Americans, on this point, would most likely agree
with him. Popular opinion, strong and constant, might sway
us momentarily—for example, as we watch wars such as that

in Yemen today, generating the greatest human tragedy since World War II. But the march of great power to its own ends would not cease, not even for a moment. We might lament the destruction by Saudi Arabian aircraft of portside cranes used to off-load food and water for the cholera-plagued victims in Yemen, but raising an effective hue and cry about the US-provided bombs that did it seems too much for us.

As this book demonstrates, however, the "nuisance value" of all those who really care is nibbling away at power, and Sir Nigel's "more" is growing. One day, perhaps a hundred years hence should the human race make it that long, our successors might be marching in a different world. This book will have been a signpost.

Col. Lawrence Wilkerson
Former Chief of Staff to U.S. Secretary of State Colin Powell
Visiting Professor of Government, College of William and Mary

Introduction

> Right is only a question between equals.
> The strong do what they can
> and the weak suffer what they must.
>
> THUCYDIDES

This is a story about a war that never should have happened—and what happened after it ended. It also is a story about the rule of international law and how that law is undermined when states ignore it. Yet above all, this is a story about a persistent issue the global community needs to address: how to give international law greater meaning—and meaningful teeth—to protect the people it was written to protect.

I spent the summer of 2016 in Vietnam conducting field research about the extent and impact of civilian exposure to unexploded ordnance and Agent Orange during and after the Vietnam War. Vietnam is a compelling case study, exemplary of the larger and global issue of state responsibility for not only wartime atrocities but especially post-war cleanup and reparations. My research has involved a.) the compilation of both quantitative and qualitative data, including interviews with U.S. war veterans and Vietnamese staff of non-governmental organizations; b.) the review of U.S. and Vietnamese government databases, identifying the location and quantity of Agent Orange sprayed during the Vietnam War; and c.) assessing the short- and long-term health implications associated with exposure to live ordnance and toxic herbicides.

I made site visits to Vietnamese and international organizations throughout the country, conducting interviews with staff to learn about the experiences of victims of chemicals and bombs, and to understand the involvement and roles of the U.S. and Vietnamese governments in post-war cleanup and reparations. The organizations I visited included the Vietnamese Association for Victims of Agent Orange, Vietnamese Women's Union, Veterans for Peace, and Project RENEW, the latter two groups having been founded by returning U.S. veterans.

I conducted reviews of news stories and journal articles pertaining to U.S. involvement in Vietnam, civilian exposure to unexploded ordnance and Agent Orange, and the gender- and transgenerational effects of these exposures. Finally, I researched United Nations databases and reviewed numerous international treaties and conventions pertaining to state responsibility for the legacy and effects of war.

Two individuals proved to be particularly helpful in my research. One is Chuck Searcy, an American Vietnam War veteran and the co-founder of Project RENEW, a Vietnamese organization committed to neutralizing the effects of war. RENEW staff physically—and often perilously—remove unexploded ordnance from provinces that were heavily bombed during the war and conduct outreach programs to educate local communities about the existence and dangers of unexploded bombs. Searcy, whose work is recognized by the U.S. Congress, was with U.S. military intelligence in Saigon during the War, and is now a full-time resident in Vietnam as well as a leading expert on the aftermath of the conflict.

The other individual is Dr. Jeanne Stellman, Professor Emeritus at Columbia University's Mailman School of Public Health. Dr. Stellman specializes in environmental health with particular expertise in human exposure to Agent Orange and other herbicides, including those deployed by the U.S. military in Vietnam. In collaboration with her scholar husband, Steven Stellman, she obtained U.S. military records to track herbicide exposures in Vietnam, doing so in conjunction with the National Academy of Sciences and the U.S. Institute of Medicine.

My hope is that this book will contribute to the field of international human rights law in several ways. First, that the United States take responsibility for the impact of its left-behind weapons in Vietnam, and that it commits to clean up those weapons as well as make reparations to the civilians who were harmed. Second, that these findings foster greater adherence of all states to their post-war obligations for cleanup and reparations. As it stands, these matters are largely unaddressed, certainly among the lay public but too often among policymakers and throughout the international community itself. Finally, that this book foment greater compliance of states to international law. I also hope it inspires the United Nations, international non-governmental organizations, and internal state and non-governmental organizations to strengthen enforcement mechanisms to compel state compliance in general.

Ariel Garfinkel

October 2017

CHAPTER ONE

War Without End

> Only the dead have seen the end of war.
>
> PLATO

I t's common knowledge that war is hell, but only some know the hell that continues long after combat ends.

The perils of military combat are well documented. The technological and communications advances of the past century or so have captured the immediate impact of conflict on both combatant and civilian populations, shedding light on the realities of the battlefield. Walking soldiers suddenly turn into obliterated corpses when hit by an enemy mortar; a tank captain peers from his turret only to take a fatal rifle shot through the forehead; entire platoons are pinned down by days of gunfire and rockets, with only a handful of survivors, crippled and bloody; and civilians, always the civilians, become trapped in the deadly conflict that takes place in their fields and villages.

What is less known, and certainly less reported, is that the violence of war—from the immediacy of raw, physical violence to the slow burn of psychological disorders and chronic illness—typically continues long after hostilities cease, with casualties and victims mounting even decades after the end of formal conflict. The roar of battle and the clash of fighting subside into a quieter but still deadly phase. Bombs that were dropped but failed to detonate suddenly disrupt the serenity of village life when triggered by a farmer walking behind his water buffalo. Playful children find a round, rusty toy to toss to one another, only to have the small cluster bomb detonate, tearing off arms or legs, and often ending their young lives.[1] But the most profound impact of war is silent, borne by the victims left with lifelong sorrow and pain: mothers whose sons never returned; children whose fathers can no longer provide for the family; families with little or no economic means to feed themselves due to destroyed homes, burned fields, and missing family members; and the permanently impaired, particularly the families whose infants continue to be born with gruesome deformities due to the permanent alteration of their parents' and grandparents' DNA by exposure to chemical defoliants.

Over the last several decades, the international community has developed codes of conduct for not only wartime and post-war responsibilities but for other areas of human rights as well. A key test of the efficacy of this international framework is how well states fulfill their obligations for post-war reparations and cleanup of unexploded ordnance (UXO), munitions, and chemical weapons that typically continue to maim and kill civilians for years following armed conflict. While international standards such as the 1949 Geneva Conventions and Additional Protocols have established long-standing rules governing armed conflict, state responsibility for the removal of war remnants and redress for innocent civilians is often ignored. When legal obligations go unenforced, the responsibility for cleanup after war is typically left to the willingness of the offending state, reflecting either altruistic intention or a desire to secure positive world standing. But neither motivation has historically been proven sufficient to compel warring parties to accept their responsibilities during and after war.

International treaties regarding the legacy of war do exist, but with limitations in their ratification, implementation, and enforcement. It is not uncommon, for example, for states to outright refuse to ratify treaties, or to ratify but fail to implement them. This bears particular relevance to state obligations in the aftermath of war, notably the cleanup and removal of harmful and even lethal weapons left on foreign soil, and reparations to innocent civilians injured by those weapons.

A striking example of ongoing post-war harm is the Vietnam War, the term applied to the U.S. presence in Vietnam starting in the early 1960s and lasting until the departure of U.S. combat troops in 1973. (For the purpose of this book, the term "War" shall refer to the Vietnam War). During this period the United States deforested large areas of Vietnam with highly toxic chemical defoliants and, from 1965 to 1973, dropped more than five million tons of ordnance across the country.[2] When the United States military left Vietnam in 1973, after a decade on the battlefront, it left behind thousands of tons of undetonated explosives on Vietnamese soil that continue to maim and kill civilians to this day. Moreover, residual levels of toxic herbicides remain in the environment with effects that still impair the health of the Vietnamese people, including pregnant women, infants, and children.

American engagement in Vietnam presents a poignant case regarding the application of international law. Prior to the end of the War, few treaties addressed post-war cleanup. While international standards have developed in subsequent years, compliance with their mandates is often ignored.

After World War II, France reclaimed its colonial toehold in Vietnam as the defeated Japanese departed. But Viet forces soon launched a rebellion against French occupation, and the Chinese supported their struggle by placing soldiers on its border with northern Vietnam. By 1949 the struggle had turned into a conventional anti-colonial conflict, known as the French Indochina War.

The years following this conflict introduced changes in government leadership and occupation in Vietnam, effectively splitting the country in half between forces claiming self-governance and forces siding with colonial powers seeking to retain control. In 1954, the Geneva Accords ended the Indochina War by dividing Vietnam along the 17th Parallel. The North became the Democratic Republic of Vietnam

Timeline of U.S. Involvement in Vietnam

YEAR	EVENT
1959	First American deaths in Vietnam (2 military advisors).
1960	United States increases advisors (from 327 to 685).
1961	First American combat death.
1962	U.S. begins spraying herbicides to defoliate major swaths of South Vietnam.
1963	Vietnamese Buddhist monks self-immolate to protest war.
1964	Gulf of Tonkin Resolution passes Congress, giving President Johnson power to take any actions deemed necessary to defend South Vietnam from Viet Cong forces. This was also called the Blank Check.
1965	U.S. combat troops arrive in Vietnam. An extensive carpet bombing campaign known as Operation Rolling Thunder is authorized by President Johnson.
1965	First mass anti-War demonstrations in the United States.
1968	My Lai Massacre: American soldiers murder hundreds of civilians.
1969	Peace talks begin in Paris with representatives from the United States, South Vietnam and the NLF (Northern Liberation Front).
1969	President Nixon announces "Vietnamization," a plan for the U.S. to train South Vietnamese troops so they can implement roles that were performed by American troops.
1971	Congress votes to withdraw U.S. troops from Vietnam by year's end.
1973	Mutual exchange of POWs.
1973	Official end of the U.S. role in the War (last U.S. soldiers leave, but military advisors and some Marines remain).
1975	The North Vietnamese take over Saigon, signaling the end of the War.

Source: *Vietnam War Statistics and Facts, 25th Aviation Battalion website; Hatfield Group.*

under Ho Chi Minh, and the South became the Republic of Vietnam. But this division only led to further conflict as the new North and South Vietnam fought for sovereignty over the entire country. Ho Chi Minh's forces sought to liberate all of Vietnam from foreign domination, and U.S. forces arrived to protect South Vietnam and greater Southeast Asia from what they viewed as a Communist takeover of the region.

American troops arrived in Vietnam near an airbase in the central coast city of Da Nang on March 8, 1965, and they would stay in the country for the better part of a decade. The perfect storm of events that exploded into the Vietnam War brewed long before the 1960s, an ultimately deadly stew of lingering ideological and political anxieties festering in the aftermath of World War II and especially the Cold War.

U.S. bombing campaigns in Vietnam began shortly after President Johnson authorized *Operation Rolling Thunder* in February 1965, following the approval of the Tonkin Gulf Resolution.[3] The bombing campaign lasted until 1973,[4] which marked the departure of the last American combat troops from Vietnam and the official end of U.S. role in the War. American military advisors, including some Marines, would remain in-country for another two years, when the 1975 takeover of Saigon by the North Vietnamese signaled the actual end of the long-term conflict over regional control.[5]

In its decade of participation in the War, the U.S. dropped an estimated 7.66 million tons of bombs on Indochina[6] (Vietnam, Laos, and Cambodia), three times the amount deployed in Europe and the Pacific combined during World War II.[7] Of the 5 million tons dropped on Vietnam itself, a notable percentage failed to detonate—estimates put the range at 10% to 30%[8]—and they continue to maim and kill civilians today. According to reports from the Vietnamese government, even after years of de-mining efforts, ". . . 350,000 to 800,000 tons of bombs and mines remain, including high explosive bombs, shrapnel bombs, penetration bombs, missiles, mines, cannon warheads and other explosives."[9] The U.S. also buried landmines and other ordnance throughout Vietnam, many of which never detonated and remain live, often exploding upon human contact. The injuries and deaths that continue to occur remain largely unrecognized by the international community, now more than 40 years after the end of the Vietnam War.[10]

In addition to the unprecedented deployment of ordnance, the U.S. saturated some 4.5 million acres of the Vietnamese countryside[11] with 18 million gallons of toxic herbicides.[12] This spraying directly exposed an estimated 4.8 million Vietnamese people to dioxin, a derivative compound in Agent Orange regarded today as one of the most toxic substances known to science.[13] Dioxin adversely impacts humans in two ways: through direct exposure, which produces serious transgenerational effects by altering human DNA, and by indirect exposure through environmental contamination of crops and seafood.

Given the nature of war, there is variation among authoritative sources about the actual number of military and civilian deaths. Estimates of deaths among the Viet Cong range from 950,765[14] to 1,100,000;[15] estimates of deaths among the army of the Republic of Vietnam range from approximately 200,000 to 250,000[16] and according to some sources up to 313,000.[17] The range of civilian deaths is even wider, reflecting U.S. government estimates of 30,000,[18] scholarly estimates of 405,000,[19] and even as high as 2 million according to other scholars.[20] Various authoritative sources put the number of American military deaths at a minimum of 58,000.[21]

In a dramatic and intense period during early 1973, fomented largely by widespread anti-War sentiment on the part of the American public, the United States government decided to exit Vietnam quickly. It removed all of its combat forces, all of its diplomatic representation, and dismissed many of its South Vietnamese allies. But what the U.S. did not remove was the deadly munitions and herbicides it had dropped. Its unexploded bombs would lay buried in Vietnamese soil and lethal chemical residue of herbicides would percolate through Vietnamese waterways for decades to come, maiming, killing, and sickening entire generations.

Ultimately the cost of war is not to be measured in terms of adults or children, soldiers or civilians, women or men, but by its impact on human lives altogether; the pain and suffering of the wounded and permanently impaired, the deaths of its victims and their grieving families, and the broken lives of those harmed forever by its continuing impact.

CHAPTER TWO

Fifty Years of Bombs

> [Landmines] are the menace that never goes away.
> Pol Pot always said the landmine was the perfect
> soldier. You don't have to feed it. You don't have to
> pay it. It just lies in wait.
>
> BRENT STIRTON
> *South African photojournalist*

Substantial anti-Communist resolve and no shortage of bravado led the United States to unleash a greater array of military ordnance on Vietnam than the world had ever seen before. Perhaps nothing epitomizes U.S. intentions at the time more than the now-infamous 1968 statement of Air Force Chief of Staff, General Curtis LeMay: "We're going to bomb them back into the Stone Age."[1]

The 7.66 million tons of ordnance the U.S. dropped throughout the narrow, serpent-shaped nation and its neighbors included a potpourri of explosives such as cluster bombs, missiles, grenades, landmines and more. Various military terms are used to describe these types of ordnance. *Explosive remnants of war* (ERW) is an umbrella term that encompasses all types of explosive ordnance from war—artillery shells, grenades, mortar shells, rockets, and missiles—regardless of whether or not they have detonated.[2] *Unexploded ordnance* (UXO) are a subset of ERW; the term refers to those munitions that were "launched, dropped, or otherwise used but have not exploded as intended."[3] The following table lists the military terms used for these devices.

Relevant Military Terms

Ordnance	All types of military supplies, ranging from weapons and explosives to vehicles, aircraft, and artillery.
Munitions	General term for ammunition and armaments (explosive, chemical, nuclear).
UXO and ERW	Unexploded ordnance (UXO) refers to all undetonated explosive weapons (bombs, shells, grenades, mines, cluster bombs), while "explosive remnants of war" (ERW) includes weapons detonated as well as undetonated.
Cluster bombs	Air-dropped or ground-launched explosive weapons that release "sub-munitions" or "bomblets" designed to kill human targets or destroy vehicles and equipment.
Landmines	Explosive devices concealed under- or above-ground to disable or destroy human and other targets when triggered by pressure or a trip wire.
Grenades	Small bombs thrown by hand of three major types: fragmentation (lethal fragments), concussion (explosive power), and anti-tank.
Missile	A self-propelled precision-guided munition (ballistic, cruise, or surface-to-air).
Rocket	An unguided missile shot into the air.

Sources: These terms have been selected because of their relevance to the Vietnam War, and defined by the author based on U.S. military records and common usage from a variety of sources including United Nations Mine Action Service (UNMAS) and Human Rights Watch.

Of the combined ERW used by the U.S., the majority consists of cluster bombs, grenades, missiles, shells, and rockets.[4] Cluster bombs contain hundreds of small bomblets the size of baseballs, and are released by aircraft or deployed on the ground via rocket launchers, artillery, and combat vehicles.[5] During the War, cluster bombs were typically deployed by the Air Force on fixed-flight paths, often as a means of clearing space for the spraying of Agent Orange. Because of the manner in which they were dropped, unexploded cluster bombs are usually found in groups; if one is discovered, there are likely several more nearby.[6] Each of the hundreds of bomblets within a cluster bomb is relatively small, but contains thousands of pieces of shrapnel. The bombs are designed to explode several feet from the ground, dispersing their razor-sharp shrapnel over several square meters to maximize their destructive impact on humans.[7]

The release of cluster bombs from an aircraft is triggered by the spinning of a dispenser that determines the pattern in which the bombs fall, as well as their orientation to the ground. The bombs fall at the rate of 125 feet per second, exploding with the intensity of a pistol bullet and capable of maiming or killing anyone within their radius.[8] Whereas landmines usually maim rather than kill, cluster bombs are more likely to kill and cause multiple deaths.[9] But a significant percentage of these ordnance did not detonate as planned, remaining live and lethal after having penetrated the soil and waterways where they remain today.[10]

Of the array of ordnance deployed in Vietnam, an estimated 10% – 30% did not detonate due to malfunction, and have remained live and deadly for more than 40 years. Cluster bombs, which Wyatt Olson of the U.S. military's independent newspaper calls the "the demon seed of modern munitions,"[11] comprise a significant percentage of the UXO remaining in Vietnam.[12] Their prevalence, size, and occasional failure to explode, make them—along with unexploded grenades—the leading cause of UXO-related injuries and deaths since the end of the War.[13] Sprinkled throughout the country, these unexploded munitions lie quietly buried in family rice fields and backyard gardens, or scattered in forests, bamboo groves, and other areas including children's footpaths to school.[14] Local people often mistake these life-threatening devices for rocks—"rocks" that explode upon contact, killing or maiming farmers in their fields or children at play.[15]

Since the departure of the U.S. military from Vietnam in 1975, more than 100,000 Vietnamese civilians have been injured (67,077) or killed (38,958) by UXO and landmine explosions as of 2013.[16] Other reports place these figures at comparable or even higher levels, including the Vietnam Ministry of Labor, Invalids, and Social Affairs, which lists 66,000 UXO-related injuries alone.[17] As for the deaths attributed to UXO, the numbers are staggering: 38,958, the number of Vietnamese civilians killed in UXO-related explosions since 1975, is comparable to killing every baseball fan in the 37,949-seat stadium at Boston's Fenway

Park. Even today, the number of injuries and deaths continue to mount.

If we expand these figures to include Laos and Cambodia, which the U.S. bombed heavily as well, thousands more have been injured or killed.[18] Not surprisingly, the remaining live ordnance are ubiquitous in nature: in central Vietnam alone, they can be found on or in approximately 35% of the land, covering some 16 million acres.[19]

Altogether, so prevalent is the presence of UXO in Indochina that at the current rate of cleanup it would take three centuries to clear the land of explosives, according to Deputy Defense Minister Nguyen Chi Vinh of Vietnam.[20] This is because it is such tedious work to locate and identify so many unexploded weapons, and to safely detonate them individually requires many person hours.

For the victims of UXO explosions who are not killed upon impact, the harm is usually long-lasting and often permanent. Being maimed by UXO not only alters the physical appearance of a child or adult, but often destroys limbs and tears apart the fabric of families and even communities. The physical pain of the injury, the subsequent loss of work and related economic ramifications, challenges in accessing medical and rehabilitation services, and prolonged emotional trauma produce profound, long-lasting changes in the lives of survivors and families.

The physical impacts from UXO explosions, as noted by the International Committee of the Red Cross, include fragmentation wounds, burns, ruptured eardrums, loss of sight, and amputation of limbs.[21] For many, these physical wounds are exacerbated by future repercussions. Adults and children who have lost limbs to bombs or landmines, for instance, face a series of additional burdens including the fitting of artificial limbs, health and rehabilitation costs, and replacement of prosthetic limbs every set number of years.[22]

As is common for survivors of trauma, UXO victims typically suffer tremendous psychological stress as well. Many experience shame, depression, and even ostracism resulting from the stigma of the injury itself. While health services and counseling are usually made available to trauma survivors in more developed countries, such services are often inaccessible to many Vietnamese due to their remote location.[23]

This adversity may be further compounded by sudden changes in employment and financial status associated with the immediate injuries. The loss of fingers, hands, or limbs may significantly diminish or even ruin a person's ability to work.

Among those disproportionately impacted by UXO explosions are subsistence farmers, whose precarious economic status renders them vulnerable to challenges above and beyond the physical and psychological complications mentioned above. Even the most basic means of survival can become arduous, especially for subsistence farmers. Living and working land ridden with UXO substantially compromises their safety, such that growing and transporting crops and tilling the soil is all highly risky work.[24] Left with no alternative, farmers often remain trapped in a Catch-22 in which, dangerous as it may be, survival drives them to continue farming despite the impending dangers of unseen munitions.[25]

The areas of Vietnam most acutely affected by the prevalence of UXO are the South-central Coast and the Central Highlands.[26] Nestled in central Vietnam just south of the demilitarized zone that divided North and South Vietnam during the War, and 115 miles north of China Beach where U.S. troops set foot in the country on March 8, 1965, sits Quang Tri province. About 60% of combat fighting occurred in Quang Tri,[27] rendering it the most heavily bombed province and now the one with the highest levels of UXO in the country.[28] Hundreds of thousands of tons of ordnance were dropped in Quang Tri alone, and an estimated 83% of the land today remains littered with UXO.[29]

The UXO saturation in Quang Tri presents unique challenges, making local families more vulnerable. Endemic poverty and a hand-to-mouth lifestyle in the province often leave people with little option but to depend on unreliable and inadequate means of earning money such as scrap metal collection.[30] Ironically, much of the sought-after scrap metal comes from UXO. Andrew Wells-Dang, Senior Governance Advisor at Oxfam in Vietnam, explains that "with no other employment options, adult males living in contaminated areas search for UXO to remove from the ground and sell to local dealers. In some cases children are also involved."[31] Indeed, of the thousands of UXO-related deaths in Quang Tri since the end of the War, nearly one-third of the victims have been children.[32]

Unexploded ordnance have been devastating local families and communities since the beginning of the military conflict in numerous and enduring ways. Since the end of the War, Quang Tri has seen at least 8,000 serious UXO injuries and deaths.[33] Residential areas account for the largest percentage of UXO accidents (25%); this number drops slightly to 21.8% in rural areas, 11.8% in rice fields, and 10.8% in forests. In all of these regions, the leading cause of accidents is cluster bombs. The majority of UXO victims are youth and adults ages 16 to 35 (44.1%), followed by children ages 1 to 15 (27%), and adults ages 36 to 55 (25%).[34]

From 2000 to 2016, UXO accidents and casualties in Quang Tri noticeably declined, reflecting progress largely attributable to the clearance and risk education work of Project RENEW and its partner teams that remove individual ordnance and conduct local educational campaigns about the danger of UXO. Still, despite all of these efforts, the large number of ordnance that remains in the ground represents a greater risk in Quang Tri than that in many other Vietnamese provinces, a cruel example of the damage and harm that has continued since the U.S. departure.

The U.S. military's extensive seeding of the country with lethal devices ended on March 29, 1973, when U.S. combat troops left Vietnam and the War was declared over insofar as American troops were concerned. (Yet the War would continue for an additional two years while U.S. military advisors remained in the country, after U.S. combat forces departed).

In the immediate years following the U.S. departure from Vietnam, the health and well-being of American veterans was tenuous at best, as their return home brought with it many permanent physical and psychological wounds. Soldiers often experienced survivor's guilt, recurring nightmares and other forms of post-traumatic stress disorder (PTSD), with a significant number committing suicide. While the families of the veterans struggled to navigate through these challenges, the continuing impact of UXO on Vietnamese families and children was hardly on the radar in the United States. Moreover, attitudes in the U.S. often remained quite antagonistic to all things Vietnamese, as did the stance of the American government.

Silence in the Face of Death

For nearly two decades after the departure from Vietnam, American policymakers remained silent about the number of harmful weapons the U.S. government had left behind. Officials did not acknowledge the gravity of the problem, especially the fact that American weapons were continuing to maim and kill innocent civilians; nor did they willingly take responsibility for intervention or offer assistance to stop what amounted to a continuing, silent war long after the end of formal combat.[35]

It was not until the mid-1990s that the legacy of the Vietnam War and the ongoing violence against the Vietnamese people would be officially addressed, albeit in small and hesitant ways. Even then, the initial steps were taken not by the U.S. government but by private organizations, often headed by GIs who had fought in the War. One of the first efforts was undertaken by Peace Trees, an American non-governmental organization that arrived in the mid-1990s to plant trees in Vietnam, with the intention of repairing and strengthening relations between the two countries. However, the plethora of unexploded munitions in the ground interfered with the safe planting of trees and led the organization to refocus its work on the removal of ordnance.

The presence of Peace Trees in Vietnam helped to expose the existence of UXO and the enormity of the problem. The organization's work would bring about a change in the discourse and treatment of the legacy of the War, establishing the imperative not only to acknowledge the existence of the UXO, but also to call for their removal. With growing knowledge of the UXO threat and its magnitude, impetus developed to pressure the U.S. government into supporting the removal of ordnance from several acres of land, an act that symbolized the first U.S. acknowledgment of the problem it had created and then ignored for decades.[36]

Ultimately these matters served as a catalyst to generate international interest and, more importantly, to mobilize efforts to resolve the issue of UXO. This attention in turn began to pressure the United States to give even more consideration to the impact of its remaining weapons, and also to start actively acknowledging the enormity of the war still being waged beneath the waters and soil of Vietnam.

From that point forward, the idea of responsibility for UXO cleanup in Vietnam became a viable consideration on the American national policy table. The connection between U.S. ordnance and ongoing Vietnamese injuries and deaths had at last been established and U.S. culpability confirmed, at least enough to break through the political and policy resistance of prior decades.[37]

At that point the U.S. State Department began to support some UXO clearance efforts.[38] The beginning of active U.S. involvement in these efforts began in 2007 with the State Department's Humanitarian Office, with over $200,000 provided for a UXO risk-safety program in conjunction with Peace Trees.[39] More recently, between 2014–2017, the State Department promised $50 million to help bring closure to the UXO problem in Quang Tri province and to create successful management models to implement in other areas of Vietnam. Project RENEW then received an initial 3-year budget of $7.8 million of that total.

According to U.S. veteran Chuck Searcy, now a resident of Vietnam and a major player in bringing matters to the attention of U.S. officials, "This was the start of an approach to an end-game, that is to say real closure and an effort to assist Vietnam to develop the capacity to manage [the UXO] problem for future years. Within the next decade, the U.S. should be able to step back and say 'we finally assisted the Vietnamese and began to do what we should have done 40 years ago'."[40]

Yet, despite such optimism, U.S. financial contributions remain exceptionally modest compared with the actual need for UXO clearance and against the material capacity of the U.S. to engage in more serious cleanup and remediation. In 2012, for example, the Vietnamese Deputy Prime Minister, Nguyen Thien Nhan, estimated that UXO clearance in Vietnam would require $10 billion and another hundred years to accomplish at the current rate of progress. Others, as indicated, have estimated triple that amount of time for complete removal.[41] In order to make a substantial impact, the U.S. State Department would need to make far more substantial contributions.

Future progress may depend on Senator Patrick Leahy of Vermont, who has been effective in encouraging Congress to allocate money to the State Department in support of UXO clearance. In addition to Senator Leahy, Senators McCain, Webb, Harkin, and former-Senator John Kerry have also demonstrated support to varying degrees, although Leahy has by far been the most instrumental.[42]

The U.S. has also contributed to UXO clearance in other ways, including capacity-building with the Vietnamese Ministry of Defense. In addition, the State Department funds Golden West Humanitarian Foundation programs in mine-impacted countries, and contributes to general development work throughout Vietnam.[43]

The years of silence on the part of the United States had left the Vietnamese government little choice but to take whatever remediation action it could afford. Searcy notes that the Vietnamese government "put a lot of money into their own budget [for clearance]" and that "in Quang Tri there is now a good response system and rehabilitation system for victims of UXO."[44]

Above all, Project RENEW has played the key role in UXO clearance in the countryside. Committed to "restoring the environment and neutralizing the effects of war," Project RENEW is located in Quang Tri province and operates three programs: the physical removal of UXO; community education about the identification and dangers of unexploded ordnance; and a victim assistance program providing prostheses and rehabilitation for victims of UXO explosions. The majority of RENEW's revenue comes from a mix of U.S. and other international donors, including Norwegian's People's Aid (their primary partner) and the Vietnamese government through its Department of Science and Technology; Department of Health; Department of Foreign Affairs; Provincial Military Headquarters; and the Office of Province People's Committee.

Project RENEW's removal team follows the procedures of international humanitarian groups to help ensure safety. In recent years the organization has removed more than 50,000 UXO from gardens, rice fields, plantations, and roadsides in Quang Tri.[45] Within the past year alone, RENEW received more than 600 calls from local families reporting discoveries of ordnance.[46]

As shown in the following graph, there was a measurable increase over recent years in the number of UXO discovered and reported by local people to Project RENEW's teams for timely and safe removal.

UXO Clearance Activity in Vietnam Over a Five-Year Period

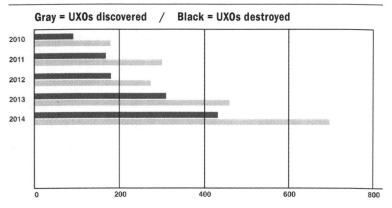

Gray = UXOs discovered / Black = UXOs destroyed

Project RENEW's victim assistance staff works closely with hospital and health care providers on incidence and outcomes of victims of UXO explosions. All amputees fitted for prostheses also receive training by health care professionals in the use and care of artificial limbs, as well as regular checkups and counseling on the need for replacement of the prostheses. RENEW is one of the key organizations in Vietnam committed to UXO clearance and victim assistance and, since 2008, its staff have fit 1,100 people with prostheses, with nearly that many more still on the wait list.[47]

For a wealthy superpower—and the major protagonist who left behind weapons of destruction that harm Vietnamese civilians to this day—the U.S. government has done little about the ongoing damage inflicted by its unexploded ordnance. Children are still being maimed by cluster bombs, their parents are still dying from grenades and mines, and the full removal of remaining live ordnance at the rate of success over the past two decades will reportedly take hundreds of years more.

But explosive ordnance are not the only threat the U.S. has left behind. Significant issues remain today involving environmental contamination and birth defects resulting from the widespread chemical defoliation by the U.S. Air Force during the War, a topic to which we now turn.

CHAPTER THREE

Herbicide Cocktails, Cancers, and Birth Defects

> If Agent Orange contaminated with dioxin were sprayed today over inhabited rice fields as it was in Vietnam back then, it would likely be considered a war crime.
>
> SENATOR PATRICK LEAHY

From 1962 until 1972, the U.S. Air Force sprayed millions of gallons of herbicides throughout Vietnam[1] with the dual purpose of destroying crops that the Viet Cong might utilize, and removing forest cover to make their presence more visible to spotter planes and airstrikes.[2] Nearly 70% of this massive chemical downpour was Agent Orange,[3] named for the color band of its storage barrels.[4] While estimates of herbicide use vary, Dr. Jeanne Stellman and her team at Columbia University place the volume sprayed at more than 20 million gallons.[5]

The spraying targeted three primary areas of Vietnam: the southern regions near the Bien Hoa and Phu Cat air bases; the central provinces near the Da Nang air base; and

Spraying of Agent Orange, Operation Ranch Hand Mission

Source: *War Remnants Museum, Ho Chi Minh City*

along much of the Ho Chi Minh Trail, a network of paths stretching the length of the country and used by the North Vietnam troops to transport soldiers and supplies to the South. The defoliants blanketed a substantial portion of the land in southern Vietnam, and as much as 34% of the targeted areas were sprayed more than once—some of them numerous times (see map on page 30).[6]

The Air Force conducted the spraying in so-called *missions* under the code name Operation Ranch Hand, carrying out a total of 20,000 missions that were often timed with the harvest cycle.[7] While Agent Orange was sprayed in about two-thirds of the Ranch Hand missions, it was only one of a rainbow spectrum of poisonous herbicides used. Agent White was the

Locations of Herbicides Sprayed in Vietnam

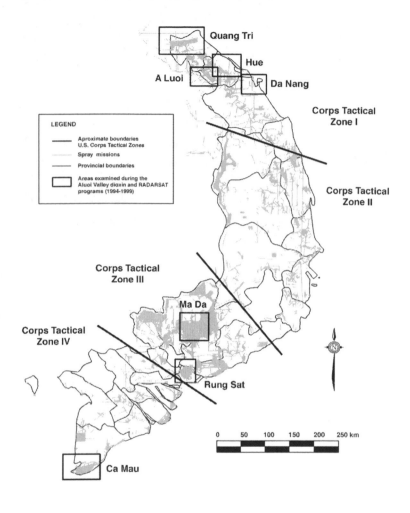

Aerial herbicide spray missions in Southern Vietnam, 1965 to 1971

Source: *U.S. Dept of the Army*

second most-used defoliant, followed by Agent Blue, used primarily for vegetation destruction (as opposed to trees). Agents Pink, Green, and Purple were also used, particularly during the early years of the War, but in smaller quantities.[8] Collectively, these defoliants were sprayed in quantities up to 50 times the concentrations recommended by their manufacturers.[9]

Often executed within days of each other, the spraying missions continually exposed Vietnamese soldiers and civilians alike to the toxic chemicals. Between 1962–1972, 3,181 villages were sprayed with the defoliants,[10] exposing some 4.8 million men, women, and children to their harmful effects.[11] Stellman's research team found that 1 million Viet Cong soldiers were exposed[12] in addition to the Vietnamese civilians. Moreover, an estimated 2.8 million American troops on the ground were exposed as well, a collateral side effect whose far-reaching consequences would not begin to be understood until decades after the War.

The spraying missions cast a wide shadow of destruction. But unlike the deployment of ordnance that comes announced by loud explosions, the peril of defoliants is more silent and more insidious, their unseen toxins penetrating the environment and food chain for years.[13]

Dioxin: A Deadly Killer

The most pernicious of these silent killers was dioxin, also known by the chemical name TCDD (tetrachlorodibenzo-p-dioxin). TCDD is a derivative compound of Agent Orange, classified as one of the most toxic substances known to science.[14] Part of a family of 75 chemicals, of which TCDD is the most toxic,[15] dioxin is a by-product of combustion or the manufacture of chlorinated chemicals.[16] According to the World Health Organization, the standard safe limit of dioxin in the blood is .07 parts per trillion (ppt), and the environmental limit in many countries typically is 1,000 ppt in soil and 100 ppt in sediment.[17] (See Table 1.) As we will see, these standards were to be ignored many times over by the U.S. military.

The effects of the ubiquitous use of this toxic agent in Vietnam were compounded by its long shelf life. Dioxin is slow to degrade in the environment, and in surface soil it can take decades to break down to its half-life (half the original concentration). According to research by The Aspen Institute, "sun will break down dioxin, so on leaf and soil surfaces it will last one to three years, depending on conditions, [whereas] dioxin buried or leached under the surface or deep in the sediment of rivers and other bodies of water can have a half-life of more than 100 years."[18]

In rivers and lakes, dioxin is persistent and accumulates in sediment. Because it's hydrophobic (water-repellent), it is typically absorbed by living organisms where it works its way up the food chain to fish and eventually to humans.[19] Moreover, just as dioxin dissolves poorly in water, it also dissolves poorly in blood, and accumulates rather quickly in fatty tissues of animals and humans.[20] In fact, over 90% of dioxin exposure comes from fish, meat, and poultry consumption[21]—sometimes in

Table 1. Conversion of Standard to Metric Measurements

STANDARD	METRIC
1 gallon	3.79 liters
1 quart	0.95 liters
1 pint	0.47 liters
1 pound (lb.)	0.45 kilograms
1 ounce (oz.)	28.35 grams
1 ounce (oz.)	28,349.5 milligrams (one-thousandth of a gram)
1 ounce (oz.)	28,349,500 micrograms (one-millionth of a gram)
0.26 gallons	1 liter
1.056 quarts	1 liter
2.11 pints	1 liter
2.2 pounds (lb.)	1 kilogram
35.274 ounces (oz.)	1 kilogram
0.035 ounces (oz.)	1 gram
0.00003527396 ounces (oz.)	1 milligram (one-thousandth of a gram)
3.5274e-8	1 microgram (one-millionth of a gram)

PPT (PARTS PER TRILLION)	PPT ANALOGIES
1 nanogram/kilogram (ng/kg) = 1 ppt	1 square inch in 250 square miles
1 nanogram/liter (ng/1) = 1 ppt	1 second in nearly 32,000 years
1 picogram/gram (pg/g) = 1 ppt	1 ounce in 7.5 billion gallons of water

Source: *http://www.csidfl.org/resources/Pharma%20Water%20Analysis.pdf*

concentrations nearly 100,000 times higher than that of dioxin found in the environment.[22]

So potent is dioxin that it continues to pose both environmental and human health risks decades after its use in Vietnam. An estimated two liters of its residue, for example, remain in the customary 208-liter (approximately 55 gallons) storage barrels at U.S. military bases, after the barrels have been emptied. Even when rinsed up to 3 times, about 20% of the residue still remains.[23] Even so-called *low residue* barrels of dioxin contain 1.25 mg, an astronomical amount when considering that a total of 85g could wipe out an entire city of 8 million people (if evenly consumed by all).[24] Barrel residue alone has led to the accidental defoliation of vegetation in civilian areas near U.S. military bases that transport the so-called *empty* Agent Orange barrels to locals for commercial use.[25]

Even the process of pumping herbicides into barrels and loading them onto aircraft for spraying missions was risky due to vapors and spillage. The National Institutes of Health has noted, for example, that during the loading of herbicide barrels into aircraft at U.S. military bases, at least four major spills occurred within a three-month period from December 1969 to March 1970, releasing a substantial amount of herbicide containing dioxin into nearby land and causing considerable contamination of soil, water, and food at the air base and surrounding area.[26]

Dioxin contamination of the environment often becomes a pernicious and virtually endless process. Dioxin can either stay in the soil or be released from burned waste products; in the latter case it binds with particles in the atmosphere, which shields it from photo-degradation. The dioxin thus stays suspended for ample time before settling, often into nearby land and surface soil.[27] Not only did the defoliant toxins affect the areas sprayed by the Air Force; they also expanded into and contaminated broader regions of the land.

Dr. Wayne Dwernychuk of Hatfield Consultants, a Canadian environmental firm whose work in Vietnam was funded by the Ford Foundation, notes that "the loss of a significant proportion of southern Vietnam's forest cover triggered a number of related effects . . . the loss of timber led to reduced sustainability of ecosystems, decreases in the biodiversity of plants and animals, poorer soil quality, increased water contamination, heavier flooding and erosion, increased leaching of nutrients and reductions in their availability, invasions of less desirable plant species . . . and possible alterations of both macro- and microclimates."[28] So much of the vegetation in Vietnam had been destroyed that natural regrowth was not viable. In the deforested areas, even new seedlings had been annihilated and soil nutrients destroyed, which, in turn, intensified erosion in the mountains and riverbeds (see photos on page 36).[29]

Even today, the contaminated land continues to harbor low levels of residual dioxin in soil, sediment, food and wildlife[30] with amounts ranging from 185,000 ppt (parts per trillion) and 236,000 ppt at the Bien Hoa and Phu Cat air bases, respectively, and as high as 365,000 ppt at the Da Nang air

Before Spraying

After Spraying

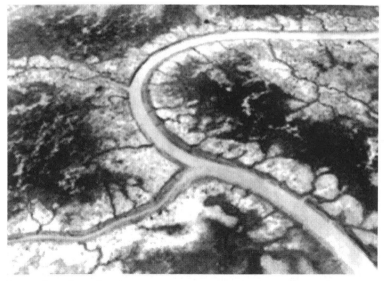

Source: *Agent Orange Record*

base.[31] As mentioned earlier, the standard international limit set by most countries cannot exceed 1,000 ppt in soil and 100 ppt in sediments without requiring immediate remediation.[32] In the case of the Vietnam War, immediate remediation was not an option due to the ongoing hostilities, and it was then rendered impossible altogether by the abrupt evacuation of the U.S. military, which left behind numerous dioxin-contaminated areas and storage supplies.

The historical record of the War establishes that from the mid-1960s until the early 1970s, Vietnam effectively became a laboratory for a massive experiment on human life. Both Vietnamese and American combatants, as well as millions of civilians, were directly exposed to one of the most toxic chemicals known to humankind, leaving the impact to be revealed only decades later.

Early Knowledge of Toxicity

At the time of their use in Vietnam, the toxicity of Agent Orange and the other herbicides were quite well known to the manufacturers. As noted by Stellman, Agent Blue had been linked to a variety of cancers in rats; Agent White was a proprietary product of Dow Chemical containing *hexachlorobenzene*, a probable human carcinogen; and Agent Purple had even higher levels of dioxin than Agent Orange.[33]

Statements made some years after the War in class-action lawsuits, including the testimony of chemical company officials themselves, reveal that manufacturers were aware of serious adverse health consequences associated with dioxin as early as the 1950s, long before the start of the Vietnam War. During a lawsuit by Monsanto workers, for example, the company's medical director, Dr. R. Emmet Kelly, acknowledged that dioxin "is the most toxic compound ever experienced. It presumably is toxic by skin contact as well as by inhalation . . . even trace amounts of this (200 parts per billion) have caused chloracne [skin lesions] . . ."[34]

It would be decades, however, before independent scientific studies would document the potency of this lethal chemical agent. Researchers would find that dioxin binds strongly with intracellular receptors in the human body, easily accessing the nuclei of cells where DNA is located. This, in turn, can alter the DNA code that produces enzymes, hormones, and proteins and as a result, can cause severe fetal deformities and chronic diseases.[35]

A 2009 study by the U.S. Institute of Medicine found "evidence of association between exposure to dioxin and five illnesses: soft tissue sarcoma, non-Hodgkin's lymphoma, chronic leukemia, Hodgkin's disease, and chloracne . . . [as well as] evidence suggesting an association with prostate cancer, multiple myeloma, amyloidosis, Parkinson's disease, heart disease, hypertension, type 2 diabetes, cancer of the larynx and lung, and spina bifida."[36] Professor Arnold Schecter of the University of Texas/Dallas notes that "although the health or epidemiology research from Vietnam on cancer and birth defects is not considered conclusive by Western scientists, it has been shown from other studies that dioxins are toxic and can cause . . . cancer, immune deficiency, nervous system damage including lower IQ and emotional problems, endocrine disruption including diabetes, thyroid problems, sex hormone disorders, liver damage, reproductive and developmental pathologies, and death from heart attacks in highly exposed workers."[37]

Alongside these documented impairments and diseases, other research has pinpointed an association between dioxin and birth defects in the children of adults who were exposed during the War. Research sponsored by the U.S. National Institute of Environmental Health Sciences (NIEHS) concluded that dioxin exposure in Vietnam was responsible for more than 500,000 birth defects in the children of exposed adults.[38] Led by Professor Michael Skinner of Washington State University, the NIEHS research team found that dioxin exposure imprints changes in the patterns of sperm across generations of descendants, so much so that were dioxin completely removed from the environment today, its impact would still continue to cause disease and birth defects for generations to come.[39]

Considering the long-term effects of herbicide exposure on humans, it should not come as a surprise that the rate of birth defects in Vietnam quadrupled since the War, and mostly in regions where Agent Orange was sprayed or stored.[40] Researchers at the Hue Medical School in Vietnam found remarkably high numbers of children in Cam Lo, near one of the U.S. air bases, with several disabilities listed by the U.S.

Veterans Administration as congenital disorders in the offspring of female veterans.[41] Similarly, a joint study by Vietnamese and Japanese scientists found a high rate of infertility in women in two sprayed communities in Cam Lo, as well as highly elevated levels of dioxin in breast milk.[42] Moreover, as early as the 1970s, Arnold Schecter's team found elevated levels of dioxin in human milk samples, as well as in seafood from southern Vietnam where Agent Orange spraying was widespread,[43] and Dr. Jean Grassman of Brooklyn College in New York has noted that "women pass their exposure to their children both in utero and through the excretion of dioxin in breast milk."[44]

Transgenerational effects are the long-term consequence of dioxin exposure, but the short-term consequences are nearly immediate. An estimated 400,000 Vietnamese, for example, died as a result of exposure to the chemical sprays.[45] The Vietnamese Red Cross estimates that "up to three million Vietnamese have suffered health effects from dioxin exposure, of whom at least 150,000 are children . . ."[46] As for U.S. troop exposure, the Veterans Administration presumes that "any of the 2.8 million U.S. veterans who had 'boots on the ground' in Vietnam were exposed to dioxin-contaminated herbicides, including Agent Orange."[47]

As evidence continues to mount, researchers now consider the variety of chemical defoliants used during the Vietnam War to pose unacceptable risks to human health, both then and today. But this knowledge and the consensus regarding their lethal effects were not attained quickly, largely because of debate over the link between herbicide exposure and adverse health outcomes, and especially because of lack of actual proof regarding causality. Researchers know, for example, that as a group, victims of dioxin exposure experience higher rates of birth deformities, but they cannot prove that any one individual case is due to dioxin exposure itself.

Early Knowledge Denied

With no way for researchers to prove direct causation—what scientists call a *dose-response* relationship—between dioxin exposure and health outcomes, U.S. policymakers simply denied that Agent Orange was the cause of the high number of diseases, deformities and health complications, whether they occurred among Vietnamese civilians or returning American soldiers. It would take years before sufficient evidence accumulated to establish the link to Agent Orange exposure. Even when U.S. officials did finally acknowledge the impact of exposure on troops who had served in Vietnam, they continued (and still continue) to ignore the impact that dioxin exposure had (and continues to have) on the families and children of Vietnam.

The dissonance between what scientists knew and what U.S. policymakers accepted was not unlike today's politically motivated denial of global warming. Even as scholarly evidence mounted, neither the U.S. government nor the chemical companies involved admitted that these health outcomes were caused by the spraying of Agent Orange.[48] The extent of the U.S. denial about possible linkages was reflected in the cynical

Birth Deformities Believed to be Related to Agent Orange Exposure

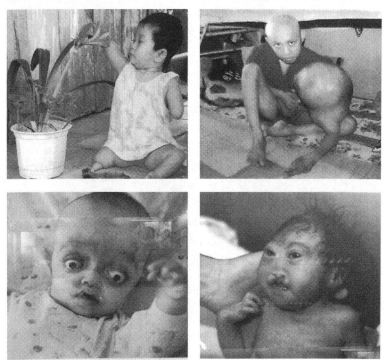

Source: *War Remnants Museum, Ho Chi Minh City*

claim of Pete Peterson, former U.S. Ambassador to Vietnam and a former Air Force pilot: "Any talk of Agent Orange is propaganda designed to extort war reparations."[49]

Despite official denials, sufficient scientific knowledge existed regarding toxic agents for the military to know that humans should not be exposed to them. As early as April 1970, the U.S. ordered a domestic ban on trichlorophenoxyacetic acid—(2,4,5-T), a component of Agent Orange—on the basis of its teratogenicity, including evidence of congenital malformations.[50] But the ban did not extend to use outside the U.S. as the War effort stood paramount in the thinking of those in charge. Admiral Elmo Zumwalt later noted that "because the material was to be used on the enemy, none of us were overly concerned."[51]

It was not until U.S. troops began to return from Vietnam, many with a variety of serious but unexplained health problems, that attention would turn to the possibility of a link to war-related chemical exposures. However, the U.S. government, primarily through the Department of Defense and the Department of Veteran Affairs, wanted nothing to do with what they claimed to be unsubstantiated conjecture. The policy of the federal government was that there was no evidence to link Agent Orange to the health status of returning veterans. This position, however, would change with the gathering of additional evidence.

Research Links Agent Orange to Dioxin Poisoning

In the early 1970s, Congress ordered a joint study by the Department of Defense and the National Academy of Sciences to assess the environmental and physiological effects of defoliation in Vietnam. Referred to as NAS-1974, the study relied heavily on what were known as the HERBS files (based on the term *herbicides*), an Air Force database of flight path coordinates used for Agent Orange spraying missions conducted between 1965 and 1971. The HERBS files contained flight logs of nearly 10,000 U.S. flight missions during the War, detailed written records of troop and civilian locations, and information about land and soil composition.[52] Yet as useful as the HERBS files were in providing such information about the location and targets of the missions, slight but noticeable inaccuracies in pilot records, transcription, and other information led to questions about the integrity of the data.[53]

This was to change, however, through the research of Professor Jeanne Stellman of Columbia University's Mailman School of Public Health, whose team performed a rigorous and comprehensive review of archival data from the U.S. military. While working in collaboration with the U.S. Armed Services Center for Research of Unit Records, Stellman's team re-examined the HERBS files and, in the process, discovered additional archives that had previously been overlooked. The new information included the location and movement of American troops in relation to individual Agent Orange flight paths, which enabled the team to calculate overlays of precise flight patterns with actual U.S. troop presence in the vicinity of specific spraying missions.

According to Stellman, the team thus "transform[ed] the HERBS files from a chronological listing of criss-crossing flight paths into target-related patterns of flights at different points in time,"[54] which is what was needed to assess exposure risks of U.S. troops. Moreover, in revising their data, the team found that the amount of dioxin sprayed during the time period in question was nearly double that estimated in the original NAS-1974 study.

The value of Stellman's research lay not merely in assessing the use of Agent Orange and other herbicides but in identifying the exposure risk to U.S. combatants by plotting mission data against geographic coordinates, which revealed the location and movement of troops in relation to each spraying mission. According to a study published in the journal *Nature,* the new maps indicated "whether individual soldiers or populations were likely to [have been] present in a particular zone on the day of the spraying and exposed directly, or whether they arrived later and were exposed indirectly."[55] This evidence eventually made it possible to establish an association between elevated levels of health adversities among military troops (and even Vietnamese civilian populations) who were situated along or near the documented spraying paths.

As with the exposure data about U.S. veterans, the number of Vietnamese civilians exposed would prove to be significant. The Hamlet Evaluation System (HES) established in the 1960s by U.S. advisors and South Vietnamese counterparts to compare census data and population estimates of civilian villagers was later utilized by Stellman's team to determine the number of Vietnamese civilians residing in direct spray paths. Whatever adverse health outcomes U.S. troops on the ground would have experienced from direct exposure to Agent Orange, these civilians would likely have experienced as well, and perhaps even more so since, unlike soldiers, civilian positions along the flight paths were largely fixed.

Stellman's research provided scientific validity to the health concerns of U.S. veterans by establishing links between exposure to dioxin and adverse health outcomes. This information, detailed by Stellman in widely covered Congressional testimony, served as an impetus to finally demand U.S. government acknowledgment of the problem. Government denial and inaction was no longer politically feasible, particularly given rigorous reactions to the evidence on the part of U.S. veteran groups, which was widely covered by U.S. media.[56]

The contributions by Stellman's team were to be supplemented by other research teams investigating the long-term environmental impact of herbicide spraying during the Vietnam War. The Canadian environmental firm Hatfield Consultants assessed the long-term environmental impact of Agent Orange specifically. Hatfield conducted the majority of its research in the Aluoi Valley, selected because of its proximity to U.S. air bases, to the Ho Chi Minh Trail, and to the demilitarized zone where the defoliant was sprayed extensively.[57]

Soil samples collected from the three major U.S. air bases where the herbicides had been stored revealed elevated levels of dioxin in comparison to areas of the Aluoi Valley that received only aerial applications of Agent Orange.[58] This realization led to the discovery of so-called *hotspots*, defined as locations where Agent Orange was stored, loaded onto airplanes, and frequently sprayed.[59] These hotspots were contaminated land with TCDD exceeding internationally acceptable levels.[60]

Hatfield identified 28 hotspots altogether, the majority of which were close to the Da Nang, Bien Hoa, and Phu Cat air bases, although according to Hatfield the magnitude of Agent Orange sprayed over the course of the decade suggests that "there are quite conceivably many more [hotspots]" which have yet to be discovered.[61]

Around the same time that Hatfield conducted its research, Professor Schecter and his team from the University of Texas School of Public Health also tested the soil content near former U.S. military bases, which resulted in similar findings. The Bien Hoa base outside of Ho Chi Minh City (formerly Saigon) revealed particularly high levels of dioxin in soil as well as in 19 out of 20 human blood samples from Bien Hoa residents.[62] Considering that the World Health Organization's standard limit of dioxin exposure is thousands of times less than what was found, these outcomes proved quite significant. Schecter's team surmised that the elevated levels of dioxin likely resulted from the mishandling and spillage of Agent Orange at the southern Bien Hoa base in 1970.[63]

The Hatfield research found that in more than two dozen locations in Vietnam, Agent Orange contamination remains a problem to this day. Dioxin storage had left identifiable environmental footprints, particularly in former storage facilities at U.S. military bases. The researchers thus concluded "that the pattern of dioxin contamination recorded in the Aluoi Valley serves as a model for contamination throughout southern Vietnam . . . and subsequent contamination through the food chain transfer of TCDD is expected to be highest in areas of former military installations where significantly higher concentrations of TCDD may be residing in soils, particularly as a result of herbicide spills."[64]

After decades of inaction and even denial on the part of U.S. policymakers regarding the toxic effects of dioxin exposure on humans, it seemed that science had finally prevailed. During the mid-to-late 1990s, discussions began to take place regarding the ordnance and chemical weapons the U.S. had left in Vietnam. President Bill Clinton lifted the U.S. embargo against Vietnam in 1994, which soon led to the restoration of diplomatic relations between the two countries. Soon thereafter, other research teams began to arrive in Vietnam to study dioxin contamination, and growing evidence continued to pressure the United States government to do more regarding cleanup in Vietnam.

Initial Acknowledgement Of Harms

Not surprisingly, U.S. veterans were the first subjects of government attention. The Agent Orange Act of 1991 directed the U.S. Institute of Medicine (IOM) to assess the strength of the evidence of a link between exposure to military herbicides and disease in veterans, and the feasibility of conducting further epidemiological studies. The Act also recommended that the Department of Veterans Affairs develop historical reconstruction methods for characterizing exposure to herbicides in Vietnam.[65]

In addition to compensation and assistance for U.S. veterans, both the U.S. and Vietnamese governments began to explore limited funding for dioxin cleanup projects as well as possible compensation for victims of the spraying missions in prior decades. But these responses were tardy, meager, and dragged out over a number of years. In fact, it was not the U.S. government that took the lead, but the U.S.-based Ford Foundation.

In the year 2000, Ford began to fund soil testing in Vietnam to further assess the levels of dioxin contamination and to gauge the continuing degree of human exposure. Ford additionally funded public education for Vietnamese victims of both dioxin-related birth defects as well as left-behind U.S. cluster bombs. Ford's initial efforts were augmented in 2009 by a further investment to provide health and remedial services to the Vietnamese people.

Over a period of more than a decade, the Ford Foundation contributed more than $17 million "to test for and contain dioxin-contaminated soils, develop treatments and support centers for Vietnamese who have been exposed, restore landscapes, and educate the U.S. public and policymakers," as noted by Charles Bailey, Director of the Agent Orange in Vietnam Program at The Aspen Institute.[66] Ford also funded both U.S. and Vietnamese organizations to deliver health, education, and employment services to young adults with disabilities, especially those linked to Agent Orange exposure.[67] The public leadership role played by Ford would later spur the involvement of the U.S. government, particularly Congress, regarding responsibility for cleanup and remediation programs in Vietnam. Meanwhile, the American Red Cross partnered with Ford, contributing $1.5 million to begin to assess and track dioxin hotspots in Vietnam.[68]

Over time several international bodies, including non-governmental organizations (NGOs) and other major U.S. foundations, joined in efforts to address the critical problem of dioxin contamination. Among others, these included UNICEF, the United Nations Development Program (UNDP), the Bill and Melinda Gates Foundation, and The Atlantic Philanthropies.[69]

All such private efforts notwithstanding, it would take the U.S. government several more years to act and help remediate the dioxin exposure of millions of Vietnamese civilians. Not only was the U.S. response tardy, it was tepid. It was not until 2007 that the appropriation of funds for Agent Orange and dioxin remediation began. Congress allocated $3 million for cleanup of dioxin-contaminated sites in Vietnam, and to support community health programs near those areas.[70] Other small allocations would follow, guided in part by a bilateral advisory committee of the Environmental Protection Agency (EPA) and a Vietnamese government counterpart, designed to speed up the pace of action regarding dioxin cleanup.[71] The Congressional Research Service notes that "the appropriated funds for environmental remediation generally have been allocated under the State Department's Economic Support Fund account, while the funds for health and disability programs have been allocated under the Developmental Assistance account [and] the State Department has delegated responsibility for the administration and obligation of the appropriated funds to USAID."[72] Of the funds appropriated for 2007-2013, USAID allocated 81% for environmental remediation, and 16% for health and disability services. The remaining 3% of funds was not allocated by the end of fiscal year 2013.[73]

The irony of U.S. funding for a hasty cleanup, after having ignored any responsibility for dioxin contamination in Vietnam for over three decades, was that it took but meager steps. In April 2011, Congress approved $18.5 million for the fiscal year, of which $3 million was allocated toward health activities.[74] The table below shows Congressional expenditures for Agent Orange and dioxin remediation throughout Vietnam from 2007 to 2014. Total U.S. contributions for this period were $130.3 million, an unjustifiably small amount for so large and serious a problem (see Appendix C).

While this was arguably *too little, too late,* it is questionable whether the U.S. would have provided any funding at all were it not for the insistence of Senator Patrick Leahy of Vermont. Leahy was the one who earmarked items in the federal budget for Vietnamese people with disabilities. Wary of potential criticism that dioxin exposure cannot be determined as the cause of any particular person's disability, Leahy's language noted that "such assistance [be provided] regardless of cause."[75] Under his watchful eye, U.S. funding for the Vietnamese would continue to be provided, albeit limited. According to USAID, starting "with a program financed by the Leahy War Victims Fund, the U.S. government has provided over $60 million in

Table 2. Congressional Appropriations for Agent Orange/Dioxin Remediation and Health-Related Activities in Vietnam

(in Millions of U.S. Dollars)

Congress	Public Law	Date Enacted	Fiscal Year	Total Amount	Environmental Remediation	Health-Related Activities
110th	P.L. 110-28	May 2007	2007	3.0	n.a.	n.a.
111th	P.L. 111-8	March 2009	2009	3.0	n.a.	n.a.
	P.L. 111-117	December 2009	2010	3.0	n.a.	n.a.
	P.L. 111-212	July 2010	2010	12.0	n.a.	n.a.
112th	P.L. 112-10	April 2011	2011	18.5	15.5	3.0
	P.L. 112-74	December 2011	2012	20.0	15.0	5.0
	P.L. 112-175[a]	September 2012	2013			
113th,	P.L. 113-6	March 2013	2013	19.3	14.5	4.8[b]
	P.L. 113-46[c]	October 2013	2014			
	P.L. 113-73[d]	January 2011	2014			
	P.L. 113-76	January 2011	2014	29.0	22.0	7.0
	P.L. 113-235	December 2011	2015	22.5	15.0	7.5
TOTAL				1303	82.0	27.3

Source: CRS research, with the assistance of U.S. Agency for International Development (USAID).

Notes: Table does not include $3.9 million allocated for these purposes by the State Department out of funds appropriated for more general uses, such as the Economic Support Fund (ESF). Appropriations made in the 110th and 111th Congress did not allocate amounts between environmental remediation and health-related activities.

a Superseded by P.L. 113-6.

b Amount based on sequestration rate of 33%: USAID reported a preliminary figure of $3.0 million.

c Allowed for the continuation of funding at levels approved by P.L. 113-6 through January 15, 2014.

d Allowed for the continuation of funding at levels approved by P.L. 113-6 through January 18, 2014.

assistance to disabled Vietnamese, regardless of the cause of the disability."[76]

The initial work of the Ford Foundation had clearly implicated the U.S. government in the contamination of Vietnam, which in turn led to a cooperative cleanup effort at the Da Nang airport, signifying the first involvement of Washington in cleaning up Agent Orange in Vietnam.[77] Rising costs and other unanticipated delays, however, prolonged remediation efforts in Da Nang until long after the start of the project in 2009. A 2014 audit revealed that the estimated project costs had risen from $33.7 million to $88 million. Meanwhile, the Vietnamese rainy season—which prolonged the excavation of soil and construction of treatment areas— led to the shutdown of a secondary treatment facility, and the need to decontaminate more soil than originally estimated introduced additional setbacks.[78] This effort continued over several years, with restoration work at the Da Nang base finally completed in the summer of 2016.

A second air base cleanup at Bien Hoa, one of the worst contaminated sites due to herbicide storage during the War, was scheduled to be completed by the end of 2017. It was estimated that the amount of soil that needed to be removed and treated at Bien Hoa, along with the Da Nang and Phu Cat sites, was "enough material to cover a football field nine feet deep."[79]

Parallel to these cleanup efforts, the U.S. provided a small amount of funding for the expansion of disability services as redress for Agent Orange victims. As tends to happen, support typically goes not directly to the victims but indirectly, through

Vietnamese organizations. The various forms of support for families, such as health and rehabilitation services, usually depend on the recipient organizations. Initially, the majority of funds for health and disability services were allocated for programs specifically in Da Nang, a major Agent Orange hotspot, but were subsequently expanded to cover disability services more broadly than in Agent Orange hotspots.[80]

In 2012, USAID approved a three-year Persons with Disability Support Program (PDSP), headquartered in Da Nang, to be implemented jointly by Development Alternatives, Inc (DAI), and Vietnam Assistance for the Handicapped (VNAH).[81] A USAID program summary reports that after two years, "nearly $900,000 in grants to 14 local partners and organizations" had been awarded.[82]

Efforts by the Vietnamese Government

The Vietnamese government had reportedly been reluctant to raise concerns that the U.S. should be doing substantially more about contamination remediation and victim compensation because of concern that such pressure could undermine a growing economic relationship between the two countries.[83] Cooperation is an issue for both Vietnam and the United States as each nation seeks to mitigate the growing role of China in the region. This mutual concern aside, the government of Vietnam has limited resources, certainly in comparison to the U.S., to clean up environmental toxins and especially to provide compensation to citizens whose lives have been permanently crippled by dioxin exposure, often inter-generationally.

Vietnam's contribution to date totals an estimated $600 million, including small monthly stipends based on individual health status.[84] On occasion, support extends to the provision of medical and rehabilitation services.[85] The government has also initiated several environmental restoration efforts, such as rebuilding mangrove forests in the Mekong Delta region and in Can Gio province near Ho Chi Minh City, designed to mitigate the impact of erosion resulting from the removal of dioxin-contaminated soil.[86] The Vietnamese government also took measures to contain the dioxin contamination at Bien Hoa, such as the excavation of a passive landfill in 2009 where contaminated soil was left untreated.[87] Such efforts, however, are generally limited fixes given their modest size.

The combined efforts of the U.S. and Vietnamese governments, particularly in comparison to the environmental and human health threats posed by dioxin contamination, pale in the face of overall need. In fact, in some respects the problems may be worsening. The Ford Foundation notes recent research revealing that dioxin is "moving into surrounding communities and up the food chain."[88]

A Long and Hard Path Forward

The longstanding threat of dioxin exposure in Vietnam clearly will not be meaningfully addressed, let alone ameliorated, at the current rate of intervention. And pressure almost certainly will be placed on the U.S. to do substantially more. The Aspen Institute, for example, has outlined four specific areas in which the U.S. should display greater commitment to address the dangers of widespread Agent Orange contamination in the country:

- Publish a strategic plan to become the basis for sustained U.S.-Vietnamese cleanup and remediation work, including prioritizing heavily sprayed provinces;
- Design and implement a health and disability program in conjunction with Vietnamese NGOs and government agencies;
- Actively seek other bilateral donors to support long-term health and disability programs as well as development assistance efforts; and
- Facilitate a Congressional review of progress and assessment of results regarding U.S. appropriations for Agent Orange efforts in Vietnam.[89]

But the key issue that has yet to surface is what the United States might owe to Vietnamese civilians whose lives and well-being have been permanently harmed by Agent Orange exposure—a potential obligation that could extend to those impacted by the tons of UXOs the U.S. dropped on Vietnam. Project RENEW's Chuck Searcy notes that inadequate attention to the plight of families presumed to be suffering from exposure to Agent Orange is the biggest weakness of U.S. aid. As he notes, "the U.S. needs to do more to help but it has never developed a truly comprehensive plan to look at appropriate solutions for Vietnamese families."[90]

The Congressional Research Service suggests that Searcy's analysis is appropriate, noting that the allocation of funds for health and disability services for victims of Agent Orange exposure "has drawn some Congressional attention" but at a very slow pace.[91]

———————

The U.S. government has done surprisingly little to address the plight of Vietnamese families whose lives have been disrupted by America's widespread deployment of chemical defoliants and unexploded weapons of war. While it has spent several million dollars in support of former base cleanup, U.S. efforts have been miniscule in the context of its substantial destruction of the Vietnamese environment, and particularly the harm to human health and lives. Moreover, the United States has never formally acknowledged responsibility for poisoning the environment and villages of Vietnam, nor has it ever provided reparations to victims of Agent Orange. In short, nearly five decades after ceasing combat, the United States has not seriously confronted its responsibility under international law for the deadly destruction it visited on the country and the people of Vietnam.

We turn now to examine relevant legal standards regarding state accountability for redress of grievance related to the exercise and aftermath of war. This assessment includes international treaties, conventions, and protocols, as well as longstanding legal concepts embodied in international law that are relevant to consideration of U.S. responsibility.

CHAPTER FOUR

U.S. Responsibility Under Treaty Law

Laws are silent in the midst of arms.
Cicero

The question of what, if any, responsibility the United States has with respect to cleanup of unexploded ordnance and chemical defoliants left in Vietnam, or reparations for victims and their families, is complex and multifaceted. As shown in previous chapters, the ongoing injuries and deaths from left-behind ordnance represent one set of factors to consider. But assessment of the U.S.'s legal responsibility for cleanup and reparations is intricate, considering the types of weapons deployed during the War; the locations of their deployment; the impact on their human targets; and, not least, the international legal standards that governed U.S. actions both during and after the conflict. If, for example, American weapons were deployed in compliance with said standards, and if their deployment was commensurate with the established duty of states to protect civilians during war time, the only legal considerations remaining would appear to be those of responsibility for cleanup and reparations. But if the international legal standards were neither observed nor met—either then or even now, given that U.S. weapons continue to harm the people of Vietnam—then the failure to comply could be relevant to international treaty standards adopted even post-war.

Global legal standards have existed for decades, some for well over a century, governing the conduct of states during war, the use of weapons, the protection of civilian populations, and responsibility for the aftermath of conflict. These standards have set global precedent for state obligations and norms of responsibility. Yet as tends to happen with bodies of law, norms change and individual state interpretations of treaty provisions can vary.

We turn now to the body of established international treaty law for the context and basis for our consideration. This chapter examines the four treaties most relevant to the analysis of U.S. responsibility mentioned above, and Chapter 5 focuses on the more general body of *customary international law*. We first review two treaties that pertain to explosive weapons: the Convention on Certain Conventional Weapons (CCW) and the Convention on Cluster Munitions (CCM). Then we analyze two treaties governing the use of chemical defoliants: the Convention on the Prohibition of Military or Any Other Hostile Use of Environmental Modification Techniques

(ENMOD) and the Convention on the Prohibition of the Development, Production, Stockpiling and Use of Chemical Weapons and on Their Destruction (CWC).

Convention on Certain Conventional Weapons (1983): Protocol V on Explosive Remnants of War (2006)

The Convention on Certain Conventional Weapons (CCW) entered into force in 1983—and was ratified by the U.S. in 1995—with the objective of restricting and banning the use of certain weapons of warfare that cause unnecessary injury or suffering to combatants or civilians. The language of the Convention itself is quite general and rather brief, but its five protocols include specific and detailed provisions (see Appendix A). Most relevant to this discussion is CCW Protocol V on Explosive Remnants of War, reportedly the first multilateral instrument to establish a clear rule that explosive munitions "must be cleared once the fighting has ended."[1]

Protocol V specifically binds States Parties to clean up left-behind ordnance and other materials after the cessation of hostilities. Its overall purpose is spelled out in the Introduction of the Convention, which recognizes that injuries to civilians typically do not end when combat ceases, and that states have a legal responsibility to protect civilians by removing explosive remnants of war. In light of the fact that the U.S. did not clean up in Vietnam, we now examine its requirements in greater detail to ascertain its relevance. The applicability of U.S. responsibility under Protocol V rests on several arguments.

Article 1(2) establishes that the Protocol applies to explosive remnants of war "on the land . . . including internal waters of High Contracting Parties,"[2] which effectively covers U.S. use of ordnance anywhere in Vietnam. In short, it covers weapons the U.S. deployed (ordnance) and where they were deployed (all geographical locations in Vietnam).

Moreover, the definition of *explosive ordnance* in Article 2(1)—conventional munitions containing explosives, with the exception of mines and booby traps—includes the major types of ordnance deployed by the U.S. during the decade of combat in Vietnam. The ordnance used were various explosive bombs and, in some instances, land mines and booby traps. Furthermore, the UXO that remain in Vietnam fit the definition of *unexploded ordnance* as defined in Article 2(2), namely "explosive ordnance that has been . . . used in armed conflict . . . may have been fired, dropped, launched or projected and should have exploded but failed to do so." The inclusion of cluster bombs—but not mines and booby traps— in the treaty language can seem subjective if not opportunistic on the part of the drafters; the distinction between these two groups of munitions has given rise to critiques of the Protocol. Some legal analysts hold that regardless of their intrinsic differences in terms of function or composition, these weapons "cannot be separated from each other on the ground"[3] as they all pose similarly harmful threats.

Particularly notable is Article 2(5), which defines *existing explosive remnants of war* as ". . . ordnance that existed <u>prior to</u>

the entry into force of Protocol V for the High Contracting Party on whose territory it exists," (emphasis added). This clearly addresses both the time in which the U.S. deployed the UXO (prior to adoption of the Protocol), as well as their location (the territory of Vietnam).

Article 3(1) clearly states that when a user of explosive ordnance no longer controls the territory after hostilities cease, the user shall "provide where feasible, *inter alia*, technical, financial, material or human resource assistance, bilaterally or through a mutually agreed third party . . . to facilitate the marking and clearance, removal or destruction of such explosive remnants of war." In other words, the Article explicitly requires the user to actively assist in the cleanup and/or destruction of ordnance. The significance of this Article is noted by the International Committee of the Red Cross, which holds that the above language is a "major improvement" from the initial text that "contained an obligation for the parties to clear explosive remnants of war in territory under their control, but merely 'to cooperate' with the other side in clearance of those weapons in other areas."[4]

Article 4 specifies that the user of explosive ordnance, even if no longer in control of the territory, must "facilitate the rapid marking and clearance, removal or destruction of explosive remnants of war." The Article further requires the user of explosive ordnance to make relevant information available to the new party in control "without delay." Similar to Article 3, Article 4 also requires specific actions on behalf of the user to assist with the clearance of UXO and to do so promptly. Accordingly, U.S. cleanup responsibility is required under these articles, for it deployed ordnance that did not explode during the War, and it also abandoned UXO upon its departure from Vietnam, which thereby continue to be *explosive remnants of war*. While the U.S. has never explicitly denied its responsibility under this provision, its forty-year silence on the matter can only be interpreted as a refusal to comply.

Article 7(1) states that each High Contracting Party has the right to seek and receive assistance from other High Contracting Parties in "dealing with the problems posed by existing explosive remnants of war," and Article 7(2) requires respective states to provide the assistance. This means that Vietnam has the right to seek and receive assistance from the U.S. for the cleanup of unexploded ordnance, and that the U.S. is required to provide said assistance upon request. To date, the U.S has yet to meaningfully comply with the requests made by Vietnamese authorities. Critics of the Protocol hold that although information sharing was widely supported in the drafting of the Protocol, the actual provision of information can be a painstakingly slow process due to political imperatives and a lack of adequate technology in rural areas.[5]

Protocol V includes a Technical Annex with suggested practices for achieving the objectives contained in Articles 4, 5 and 9 of this Protocol, and is to be implemented by High Contracting Parties on a voluntary basis. Article (1)(a)(iv) of the Annex states that when a State Party has abandoned explosive ordnance in the course of operations, it should "leave abandoned explosive ordnance in a safe and secure manner . . ." As such, this Article contains explicit provisions about post-war departure procedures and abandonment of ordnance, which is applicable to U.S. cleanup responsibility in Vietnam.

To summarize the requirements of CCW Protocol V as they apply to the U.S.:

- The Protocol covers the types of explosive weapons used by the U.S. in Vietnam;
- It includes the ordnance that remain unexploded as "remnants" of the War;
- It covers the geographical area where the weapons were used, namely Vietnam;
- The U.S. was the responsible user party that employed the weapons that remain unexploded;
- The responsible party is required to maintain or leave its remaining explosive ordnance in a safe and secure manner;
- The responsible party is required to remove its explosive munitions once hostilities cease;
- The responsible party should actively engage in all related cleanup activities; and
- If the responsible party no longer controls the territory in question, it must *rapidly* facilitate the removal and destruction of remaining explosive remnants through international cooperation, including the sharing of detailed information.

To date, the United States has fulfilled none of these obligations. This failure is now an integral part of the international legal and historical record of the War. Although the U.S. has never addressed, let alone explained, its failure to adhere to the Protocol, we can evaluate pertinent language or look for mitigating factors that might be perceived as obviating its burden of responsibility.

First, and perhaps paramount, is the fact that although the U.S. ratified both the CCW and Protocol V, neither of these instruments existed at the time of the Vietnam War. It could therefore be argued that the lapse of time from the end of the War until the U.S. ratification of the Convention (1995) and Protocol V (2009) makes their application to prior U.S. actions challenging. The question of timing illustrates an important consideration in international law, namely whether legal instruments may or should apply retroactively. In international law, it is generally accepted that retroactivity does not apply unless explicitly stated and agreed to by the relevant parties. As for the specific case of Vietnam under Protocol V, Harvard Law Professor Bonnie Docherty notes that "no past weapons treaty has imposed retroactive responsibility on user states to assist with the clearance of failed weapons."[6]

Nevertheless, the debate over retroactivity continues. Some argue that seeking to apply treaty provisions to past conflicts would "provide an important mechanism through which states and the users of explosive ordnance in past wars can work to address an existing problem."[7] It also happens that addressing the clearance of explosive remnants of war from conflicts prior to the adoption of the CCW proved to be a major point of contention during negotiations regarding Protocol V. The question of whether the Protocol should address the clearance of ordnance already on the ground, or instead apply only to future conflicts, was one of the last issues to be resolved.[8] As such, Article 7 of the Protocol allows for some flexibility in applying requirements retroactively to aggressor states, and seeks to give recourse to impacted states.

But even prior to Protocol V, precedent existed in the application of law for holding states that had committed wartime violations in the past responsible for remediation. International bodies, including the Human Rights Committee and the European Court of Human Rights, have held that states may be responsible for rectifying past actions that cause present harm.[9] Environmental law, for example, follows the principle that polluters should clean up contamination even if it predates the relevant legal instrument.[10] In this regard, Professor Docherty notes that "basic treaty law allows for the inclusion of such a provision in weapons treaties . . . including those that predate a treaty. While a treaty is not normally retroactive it can be if a different intention appears from the treaty or is otherwise established."[11] In the case of Protocol V, its intention is clear: to limit or prevent physical harm and death.

But the inescapable reality is that the unexploded weapons in Vietnam continue to kill, maim, and cause harm. For that reason alone the Vietnam War cannot, technically, be considered a past conflict, with the continuing deaths of civilians somehow overlooked by the CCW. No logical interpretation of Protocol V—established to protect civilians from post-war harm—could possibly mean that it is permissible to let people suffer and die today because of the technicality that deadly weapons were dispersed yesterday. It is in this sense—with Vietnam War-related deaths continuing more than a decade after establishment of relevant international law—that Protocol V can be applied today. In other words, the United States indeed bears responsibility for cleaning up the weapons left in Vietnam.

With the matter of retroactivity set aside, another argument against placing legal responsibility on the U.S. may be found in several ambiguous phrases in the Protocol. Assistance for clearance of explosive remnants of war, for example, should occur "where appropriate" or "as necessary and feasible." Various legal authorities note that the ambiguity of these qualifiers presents an element of discretion that could weaken the obligations.[12] Indeed, to turn responsibility for cleanup from mandatory action into a discretionary decision would weaken the entire framework, with the possible good will of individual states serving as a case-by-case substitute for legal responsibility.

Moreover, in the years following the War, the U.S. and Vietnam remained hostile actors, exchanging their weapons of war for weapons of ideology. Even if the U.S. would have assisted with the removal of explosive ordnance, there remains the open question whether it could identify areas where unexploded cluster bombs and other ordnance remain.[13]

Additional challenges persist, undermining the efficacy of the CCW. Similar to issues posed by the abovementioned ambiguous phrases, another point of contention lies in the term *superfluous injury* introduced in the Preamble. Although Protocol V does not include this particular language, the criteria for *superfluous injury* initially were left undefined and ambiguous. This issue was later resolved in 1996 by an international group of doctors who defined the term as injury that causes "permanent disability, disease other than the traumas normally caused by explosions or projectiles, virtually inevitable death in the field, a very high degree of mortality in hospital settings, or particularly severe injuries."[14] Legal experts note that the purpose of establishing such criteria was so "states at the national level and in international forums [could] assess the legality of new weapons," yet they also note that because said criteria "have not been validated internationally . . . it may not be concluded, in the current state of law, that a new conventional weapon could be considered prohibited solely because it does not meet those criteria."[15] Just as ambiguous phrases weaken convention provisions, so too, does this type of ambiguity, by providing opportunity for states to flout responsibility for cleanup.

It may be reasonable to expect ambiguities and conflicting interpretations in a complex body of international law, in this case leaving the assignment of responsibility to be ironed out on an ad hoc basis. But because the overall import of Protocol V— its clear purpose and intent at the time of U.S. ratification—is to limit or prevent the physical harm and death of innocent civilians from explosive remnants of war, any such interpretation must be weighed in the context of the very real consequences of said interpretation on people's lives. Perhaps the reason that the U.S. has never denied responsibility for the cleanup of its left-behind UXO is because America's culpability is clear.

Convention on Cluster Munitions (2010)

The Convention on Cluster Munitions (CCM), which the U.S. has never ratified, bans the development, production, stockpiling, and transfer of certain munitions altogether, and "addresses the humanitarian consequences and . . . harm to civilians caused by [such] munitions."[16] The CCM emerged in response to growing concerns about the legitimacy and impacts of cluster munitions on civilians,[17] and it states that ". . . cluster munition remnants kill or maim civilians . . . obstruct economic and social development . . . impede post-conflict rehabilitation and reconstruction . . . [and] can negatively impact national and international peace-building and humanitarian assistance efforts, and have other severe consequences that can persist for many years after use."[18] It should be noted that the call for a cluster munitions ban arose from the aftermath of the Vietnam War,[19] in response to the millions of bomblets deployed indiscriminately across the country.

We might ask what relevance the CCM holds for U.S. post-war responsibility, given that the U.S. has never ratified the Convention, but the failure to put pen to paper does not always exempt states from their global obligations. A "rogue nation," for example, refusing to accept extant rules of international governance, would not necessarily be considered exempt from prohibited or unlawful behaviors simply because it claimed that such behavior was not covered by existing treaty law. States coexist in an international community whose behaviors and relationships are governed by legal instruments and expectations.

Although drafters wrote the Convention with notable speed, several debates surfaced during the process. Proponents of the Convention reasoned that cluster munitions should be banned because they "lend themselves easily to attacks that strike combatants and civilians alike," whereas those in opposition contended that international law already suffices in prohibiting indiscriminate attacks, and that cluster munitions are not incapable of being used discriminately.[20] Instead of instituting a total ban, drafters therefore advocated for establishing restrictions based on technical reliability criteria such as a failure rate of less than one per cent. The counter argument, which eventually prevailed, was that failure rates derived from perfect test conditions rarely represented the volatile conditions of actual combat.[21]

The United States is one of the countries that opted out of signing the Convention. It was against a blanket ban, maintaining that cluster munitions can produce less collateral damage than unitary weapons. It also expressed concern that signing the Convention might obviate its ability to cooperate with, or participate in, military and humanitarian relief missions because its ships and forces often carried cluster munitions.[22]

In addition to the U.S., several other prominent nations also remain outside of the Convention, including Russia, China, Pakistan, and Israel. Legal experts note that although cluster munitions clearly have been used by non-Party states since the Convention entered into force, the stigmatizing effect of doing so often results in condemnation from the global community.[23]

While the United States has not signed this convention, several of the CCM's protocols do bear relevance to America's obligations to clean up its buried ordnance, as will become clear shortly. Moreover, given that cluster munitions are among the conventional weapons the U.S. deployed extensively during the Vietnam War, American weaponry falls under the category now widely outlawed under developing international standards.

Specific articles, in fact, assign responsibility for the cleanup of cluster munitions. Article 4(4)(a), for example, applies to cases where cluster munitions have been used or abandoned by a State Party prior to the entry into force of the Convention for that state, and whose munitions are located in areas under the jurisdiction or control of another at the time of entry into force. It requires the responsible State Party to assist the latter Party with the identification, clearance, and destruction of remaining munitions. The Article also requires the responsible State Party to assist in providing detailed information about the quantity and location of clusters to the latter State Party. As discussed previously, the U.S. kept detailed military records during the War; little doubt therefore remains that the U.S. does indeed have the capacity to provide this type of information to Vietnam.

Finally, Article 6(6) places direct responsibility on the former States Parties (in this instance arguably even the United States) to provide "emergency assistance" to the currently affected State Party (Vietnam). As such, this Article directly pertains to the role of the U.S. in Vietnam, in which case cluster munitions have now effectively become explosive remnants after entry into force of the Convention. It requires that responsible States Parties, if they are in a position to do so, "urgently provide emergency assistance to the affected State Party," an obligation that would certainly have extended to the United States had it signed the Convention. The clarity of its language notwithstanding, however, Article 6(6) includes a qualifying phrase ("in a position to do so") that diminishes its legal muscle and effectively leaves its requirements up for debate.

The following arguments may be offered as to why the U.S. bears little or no responsibility under the provisions of the CCM. Article 4(4)(a), for example, adds the caveat that the state is "strongly encouraged to provide" the various kinds of cleanup assistance mentioned. An encouragement, no matter how firmly stated, is neither a command nor an actual requirement of international law. As such, the United States, as the "responsible" State Party, can easily elect not to respond to such "encouragement."

Relatedly, the U.S. can decline to provide information about the quantities and locations of cluster munitions simply by claiming that it either no longer has such records, or that it is too burdensome to research, organize, and share them. Even if such a claim were untrue, its mere declaration leaves little room for pursuing U.S. legal obligations. While there is no evidence the U.S. has ever made such a claim, its decades-long silence on the matter does suggest that it considers itself exempt from cleanup responsibility and related obligations.

The U.S. could also claim that it offered emergency assistance to the best of its ability as required by Article 6(6) or, alternatively, that it was prepared to provide assistance but that the Vietnamese government did not respond positively so as to encourage or accept such assistance. All evidence, however, indicates that neither offer was ever made.

Aside from potential U.S. claims of exemption from the provisions of the CCM, this convention—particularly coupled with Protocol V of the CCW addressed earlier—establishes a tight and widely accepted standard that states are obligated to clean up their still-live weaponry following the cessation of hostilities. In this sense, even if a state has not agreed to refrain from future use of cluster munitions, it may be responsible for the cleanup of previously deployed weaponry, especially those that continue to kill people today.

The U.S. has expressed its recognition of the consequences of cluster munitions[24] and condemned their use in certain circumstances,[25] it has operated in general compliance with the spirit of the CCM by limiting its use of cluster munitions,[26] and it has restricted its production and trade of such weapons.[27] The reservations the U.S. has expressed about the Convention may have more to do with matters of practicality than with substantive lack of commitment to the Convention.

It is in this sense that major provisions of the CCM— particularly those regarding the responsibility to clean up buried cluster munitions—are relevant to the United States. By expressing its general agreement with the CCM, and by purporting to follow many of its key provisions, the U.S. has sought public recognition as being in support of the CCM even though it has never ratified the Convention. Indeed, the U.S. is on public record not only as being supportive of the CCM, but as being *committed* to its clean-up provisions. The Assistant Secretary of State under President George W. Bush, Stephen D. Mull, noted that "the United States is deeply concerned about the humanitarian impact of cluster munitions . . . it's an absolute moral obligation to clean up—to do everything that you can to clean up after a conflict . . . to make sure that there aren't innocent victims of weapons that are left lying around."[28]

We can summarize U.S. responsibilities as they pertain to cleanup in Vietnam under the Convention on Cluster Munitions as follows:

- Well over one hundred states have signed or ratified the CCM, but the United States has failed to do so (along with Russia, China, Israel, and Pakistan);

- The failure to put pen to paper does not always exempt states from their global obligations or allow them to flout existing standards of international governance;
- Under both Republican and Democratic administrations, the United States has expressed strong concern about the humanitarian impact of cluster munitions, and has noted that it has "an absolute moral obligation to clean up . . . after a conflict to make sure that there aren't innocent victims of weapons that are left lying around";
- By expressing its general agreement with the CCM and pledging to follow its key provisions, the U.S. has voluntarily placed itself in general support of the CCM;
- The United States is on record as being not only supportive of the CCM but also *committed* to carry out its cleanup provisions; and
- U.S. obligations remain particularly relevant given that the unexploded cluster munitions it left in Vietnam continue to maim and kill innocents today.

Thus, as a matter of stated policy and governmental practice, the United States acknowledges responsibility under the key provisions of the Convention on Cluster Munitions. This acknowledgement, without question, reflects its responsibility to clean up its left-behind cluster bombs. But the reality is that it has not complied with this responsibility in Vietnam.

In contrast to international conventions that address the use of weapons and removal of unexploded ordnance, fewer legal instruments pertain to the use and disposal of chemical weapons during and after war. Of the conventions listed in the repository of the United Nations Treaty Collection, two relatively recent conventions pertain to chemical weapons: the Convention on the Prohibition of Military or Any Other Hostile Use of Environmental Modification Techniques (ENMOD), and the Convention on the Prohibition of the Development, Production, Stockpiling, and Use of Chemical Weapons and on their Destruction (CWC). Both conventions explicitly prohibit the use of chemical weapons, but their relevance to U.S. use of Agent Orange and its possible liability for cleanup and removal of dioxin residue hinges largely upon the analysis and interpretation of relevant provisions.

It is important to note the text of the 1925 Geneva Gas Protocol, as it relates to the possible application of these conventions to the United States: "Whereas the use in war of asphyxiating, poisonous or other gases, and of all analogous liquids, materials or devices, has been justly condemned by the general opinion of the world . . . [and] to the end that this prohibition shall be universally accepted as part of International Law, binding alike the conscience and the practice of nations . . . that the High Contractive Parties, so far as they are not already Parties to treaties prohibiting such use, accept this prohibition."[29]

While this Geneva Protocol grew out of World War I, largely in response to the widespread use of deadly mustard gas on warring troops, in many ways it served as a foundational basis for these treaties that came years later.

We now turn to the related matter of America's widespread spraying of Agent Orange and the impact of its deadly dioxin.

Convention on The Prohibition of Military or Any Other Hostile Use of Environmental Modification Techniques (1977)

The Convention on the Prohibition of Military or Any Other Hostile Use of Environmental Modification Techniques (ENMOD) entered into force two years after the U.S. left Vietnam, and in 1980 the U.S. became one of now 77 States Parties to ratify. The Convention prohibits engagement with "military or any other hostile use of environmental modification techniques having widespread, long-lasting, or severe effects as the means of destruction, damage, or injury to any other State Party."[30] It was established to call attention to the negative effects that scientific and technological advances can have on human welfare and on the environment, and to "renounce the use of climate modification techniques for hostile purposes."[31] These concerns had surfaced in the international arena during the early 1970s, in the shadows of the Vietnam War and in no small part due to America's widespread use of Agent Orange.[32]

When determining the application of the ENMOD Convention to the United States' use of Agent Orange in Vietnam and potential responsibility for cleanup of residue, there are two considerations of particular relevance: first, whether the definition of *environmental modification technique* includes the use of Agent Orange, and second, whether and how the Convention applies to U.S. actions during and after the War.

Some legal scholars have held that ENMOD does not apply to the use of Agent Orange in Vietnam, although the case is by no means closed. The U.S. stance on the matter of application originated during the treaty negotiation process: the Department of Defense expressed serious reservations regarding the joint treatment of arms control and the laws of war, reasoning that the combination of these two issues might contribute to confusion and impact the treaty's efficacy. The U.S. suggested that a special interagency review be conducted to address these concerns before proceeding with negotiations, upon which policy analysts, including those from the Arms Control and Disarmament Agency—an independent agency of the U.S. government—found the U.S. position "almost incomprehensible." [33]

This caustic observation notwithstanding, the U.S. proceeded to ratify ENMOD, but continued to stand by its strongly held position that the Convention did not necessarily prevent the use of herbicides in armed conflict. According to the U.S. Air Force Commander's Handbook, "the United States has, as a matter of national policy, renounced the first use of . . . herbicides with certain limited exceptions . . . using herbicides in armed conflict requires Presidential approval." The two exceptions carved out by the U.S.—"first use" and "Presidential approval"—were accepted by some States Parties and rejected by others. Australia, for instance, noted that "environmental modification techniques are prohibited . . . [such as] defoliant chemicals,"[34] and went on to note that the use of Agent Orange, as applied by the U.S. during the Vietnam War, was now outlawed by ENMOD.

The United Nations General Assembly in 1969 (during the Vietnam War) also condemned the use of herbicides in Vietnam.[35] The General Assembly, however, is not a law-making body, and the UN Charter limits its powers to making recommendations. Its position was recognized as relevant only insofar as it pertains to the developing field of *customary international law*, a concept addressed in later chapters. While the role of the U.S. with respect to use of Agent Orange was never brought before the Security Council—which has power to make decisions about international law—it was litigated in federal court in the United States (2008). Vietnamese plaintiffs (Vietnam Association for Victims of Agent Orange) alleged that the use of Agent Orange during the Vietnam War violated customary norms and standards pertaining to poisonous weapons. The U.S. Court of Appeals, however, ruled that Plaintiffs had failed to demonstrate a violation of international law because the use of chemical defoliants was not yet a universal norm in the 1960s, and also because the U.S. had expressed reservations to the applicability of ENMOD at the time of ratification.[36]

To date, no court case or international body has ruled that ENMOD pertains to U.S. use of Agent Orange during the Vietnam War. On the other hand, no relevant parties have ruled that U.S. actions were in keeping with either the spirit of the Convention or the direction of developing international law. Given the evolving nature of international treaty law, it is important to further examine key arguments regarding the possible relevance of ENMOD.

Regarding ENMOD's applicability to Agent Orange, this chemical does seem to meet pertinent criteria as an environmental modification technique: *widespread, long-lasting,* and *severe destruction*. Its spraying was certainly widespread, blanketing over 4.5 million acres of land; it was long-lasting in that spraying continued for an entire decade and its aftermath for decades more; and it clearly upset the ecological balance, according to the U.S. State Department, causing "significant disruption or harm to human life [and] natural and economic resources . . ." such as persistent physical deformities and environmental contamination and destruction.[37]

It is also well-established science that dioxin adversely impacts the environment and human health, as referenced in Article 2 of ENMOD. Some 20 years after the entry into force of the Convention, for example, the International Review of the Red Cross concluded that the use of herbicides could "be equated with environmental modification techniques under Article 2 of the Convention."[38]

Moreover, the Convention's Understanding Relating to Article 2 also states that the list of outcomes produced by environmental modification techniques is "not exhaustive [and] other phenomena which could result from the use of environmental modification techniques could also be appropriately included,"[39] suggesting that Agent Orange fits within the definition of an *environmental modification technique*. The International Committee of the Red Cross pointedly notes that "an example of [an environmental modification technique] is defoliant chemicals used by militaries to deprive the enemy of ground cover or [to] kill food crops," and that "the United States used Agent Orange during the Vietnam War for this purpose . . ."[40] Similarly, the United Nations Environmental Program has held that "the ENMOD Convention was established as a reaction to the military tactics employed by the United States during the Viet Nam War . . . the Convention was also a reaction to the use of large quantities of chemical defoliants . . ."[41] The positions of these various experts and their institutional counterparts, coupled with Convention language stating that its list of environmental modification is not exhaustive, suggest that the application of ENMOD to the use of dioxin may not be settled law.

Whether the use of Agent Orange and dioxin in Vietnam was legal is but one issue to consider. Another key consideration is the application of ENMOD to U.S. responsibility for cleanup of Agent Orange residue. Article 5(5) requires "each State Party . . . to provide . . . assistance . . . to any State Party which so requests, if the Security Council decides that such party has been harmed or is likely to be harmed as a result of violation of the Convention."

Records indicate that Vietnam did request U.S. assistance with the cleanup of Agent Orange, and that the U.S. did respond in 2010, albeit minimally.[42] But U.S. assistance came some 35 years after the War, giving dioxin ample time to poison Vietnamese soil, contaminate water sources, and harm human health for generations through alterations in DNA. Moreover, the funding provided by Congress through the U.S. State Department came in meager amounts given the magnitude of the threat faced by the Vietnamese people. And its limited reach was narrowly focused on cleanup around former U.S. military storage units with little if any focus elsewhere.

The relevance of ENMOD to U.S. responsibility for its widespread use of chemical defoliants in Vietnam can be summarized as follows:

- The United States ratified ENMOD in 1980 and is legally bound to its provisions;
- Agent Orange and other chemical agents the U.S. deployed in Vietnam fit under relevant Convention language that prohibits environmental modification techniques, particularly those that are widespread, long-lasting, and severely destructive;
- The U.S. has pledged never to engage in "first use" of chemical agents to modify the environment during war, especially without prior Presidential approval;
- The United Nations General Assembly condemned earlier U.S. use of herbicides in Vietnam although the matter never came before the Security Council;

- The legality of the U.S. use of Agent Orange in Vietnam prior to ENMOD is not a matter of settled law, yet the Convention's cleanup requirements are considered binding on the U.S. because the impact of Agent Orange continues in Vietnam today;
- ENMOD requires each culpable State Party to assist an impacted State Party with cleanup if requested;
- Vietnam did ask the U.S. for assistance, which was both slow in coming, highly-insufficient and then terminated; and
- The nation of Vietnam continues to have poisoned soil and waterways, and human lives continue to be harmed inter-generationally through changes in DNA, resulting in severe birth defects and other physiological impairments.

Convention on the Prohibition of the Development, Production, Stockpiling and Use of Chemical Weapons and on Their Destruction (1997)

The thawing of relations between the U.S. and Russia in the 1980s and 1990s permitted the international community to focus not only on nuclear but also chemical weapons. Public knowledge and especially visual documentation of chemical attacks, particularly against civilian populations, elicited outrage from the international community, pushing to the forefront the drafting of a new agreement to prohibit the use of such highly toxic weapons.[43]

The Chemical Weapons Convention (CWC) was inspired in part by the 1925 Geneva Protocol, which prohibits the use of chemical weapons under any circumstance. It entered into force in 1993 and now has 192 States Parties, including the U.S., which ratified in 1997. It contains 24 articles that collectively "prohibit the development, production, stockpiling and use of chemical weapons."[44] The opening article establishes that never under any circumstances should States Parties engage in any military preparations to use chemical weapons.[45] The CWC also "provides for assistance to and protection of states attacked or threatened with chemical weapons . . . restrictions on the transfer of certain chemicals to non-States Parties, and sanctions in response to grave violations of its provisions."[46]

The CWC defines *chemical weapons* as "toxic chemicals and their precursors, except where intended for purposes not prohibited under this Convention . . ."[47] A *toxic chemical*, in turn, is defined as "any chemical which through its chemical action on life processes can cause death, temporary incapacitation or permanent harm to humans or animals [and] includes all such chemicals, regardless of their origin . . ."[48]

During the drafting of the Convention, the Organization for the Prohibition of Chemical Weapons noted that in order "to address the potential threat posed by chemicals, the CWC definition of chemical weapons had to be as comprehensive as possible."[49] This led to the inclusion of various classes of named chemicals and chemical compounds in appendices of the convention; yet Agent Orange and dioxin were not listed or mentioned, either by their chemical names or trade names. It could be argued that this omission was intentional, for whatever reason, although treaty appendices are often illustrative rather than comprehensive. It could also be argued that the level of dioxin in Vietnam was indeterminable or variable, although it had been sprayed in quantities exceeding international maximum exposure standards. But because dioxin impairs both humans and animals, and is associated with elevated risks of birth defects and adverse health outcomes in humans including cancers and infertility, it is widely accepted as a toxic chemical and carcinogen.[50] Moreover, neither the United States—nor any other nation for that matter—is on record as denying that Agent Orange or its dioxin derivative is covered by the CWC. Given the clarity of the Convention language, the firm scientific evidence regarding the nature of relevant chemical compounds, and the lack of any reservations expressed by states regarding dioxin, no reasons exist to doubt that this chemical is covered by the CWC.

With this established, the Convention further requires that "Each State Party undertake[s] to destroy all chemical weapons it abandoned on the territory of another State Party, in accordance with the provisions of the Convention."[51] The CWC goes on to define *abandoned chemical weapons* as "weapons, including old chemical weapons, abandoned by a state after 1 January 1925, on the territory of another state without the consent of the latter."[52] The definition of *abandoned chemical weapons* is particularly pertinent to the United States' use of Agent Orange because the chemical compound was utilized and abandoned by the U.S. well after the year 1925, and it was used and abandoned on the territory of another state (Vietnam) without its consent. Moreover, the Convention language not only requires the destruction of the chemicals themselves, but also the destruction of chemical weapons production and storage facilities "constructed or used since 1 January 1946."[53]

On its face it would be legitimate to ask whether the United States—having left Vietnam after the War, abandoned its chemical weapons and storage facilities there, and thereafter entered a lengthy period of ideological conflict with the government of Vietnam—actually had the opportunity to exercise any of its cleanup responsibilities as set forth by the Convention. It is arguable that from 1975 until the late 1980s, continuing hostilities could have limited U.S. capacity to do so. But relations with Vietnam began to improve after that period, and certainly by the time the Convention went into effect in 1997, no such rationale could have been offered for the U.S. failure to reach out to Vietnam to fulfill this responsibility.

In fact, the U.S. did not discuss cleanup on a bilateral basis with the government of Vietnam until more than a decade later, in 2010.[54] The U.S. also failed to recognize the responsibilities it held under other treaty articles. Article 3 (1)(b) of the CWC requires that States Parties must declare whether they abandoned chemical weapons production facilities and, if so, provide a plan for their destruction. While the U.S.'s abandoned facilities were under the control of Vietnam by the time the CWC went into effect, the U.S. nevertheless failed to provide Vietnam with information on the facilities it left behind, to suggest a plan of action to destroy them, and to make an offer to provide assistance with their destruction.

Moreover, the U.S., along with other States Parties, also agreed to take steps to destroy all chemical weapons within a particular time frame, starting no later than two years after entry into force of the agreement. As with the above matter, this deadline also was ignored by the United States for at least a decade.

The CWC further requires responsible States Parties to cover the costs of cleanup, both of the chemicals and their related facilities.[55] As noted in Chapter 3, although some U.S. funding for cleanup was finally appropriated starting in 2010, it was rather meager in nature, based on no analysis of overall costs, and dribbled out at the largesse of Congress—largely due to the determined efforts of U.S. Senator Patrick Leahy.

Based on the foregoing Chemical Weapons Convention obligations as they apply to the United States:

1. The CWC bans the use of a wide variety of chemical weapons, including Agent Orange and dioxin, by states engaged in armed conflict;

2. States Parties are required to destroy chemical weapons they abandoned in the territories of other states;

3. They are required to destroy storage facilities as well;
4. They must declare what they abandoned (types of chemicals weapons, locations and amounts);
5. They must assist in the destruction of chemical weapons and facilities if they no longer control the territory where said weapons and facilities are located;
6. They must carry out these responsibilities starting two years after the Convention entered into force in 1997;
7. States must pay for the costs of the cleanup/destruction of their abandoned chemical weapons.

As of this writing, the United States has fulfilled few of the legal responsibilities enumerated above. For years after the Convention went into effect, the U.S. took no action to destroy the chemical weapons or the storage facilities it had abandoned in Vietnam (points 2 and 3 above). Available evidence indicates that it failed to declare and share information regarding the weapons or to offer to assist in the cleanup of sites, weapons, and facilities (points 4 and 5 above). The U.S. also failed to meet the timeline set by the Convention (point 6 above). As for the support it did finally provide for cleanup, it was more a gesture of limited largesse than a carefully considered and formal legal act of international responsibility. Most importantly, as we will see in the next chapter, while the U.S. may not have violated these CWC provisions, the use of Agent Orange in Vietnam did violate the Geneva Protocol of 1925, which prohibits the use of chemical weapons, including "asphyxiating, poisonous or other gases, and all analogous liquids, materials or devices [and] bacteriological methods of warfare."[56] Moreover, the Geneva Protocol is accepted as an active and enforceable part of the body of international law.[57]

Nevertheless, with the CWC carrying the force of contemporary international law, it is reasonable to inquire whether any mitigating factors might have prevented the U.S. from complying with its provisions, or justified its non-compliance. In fact, only one has broken through the U.S. government's deafening silence on its duties and responsibilities under the CWC as it pertains to Vietnam: retroactivity, so far the only factor ever mentioned in scholarly literature. But in fact, with the U.S. government virtually silent regarding its obligations under the CWC as they pertain to Vietnam, the only factor mentioned in scholarly literature is that of retroactivity. As we know, the U.S. left Vietnam in 1973, at which time it abandoned the weapons now covered by the Convention, which itself went into effect in 1997. Does the CWC then apply only as of 1997, thereby possibly absolving the United States of responsibility?

On this point the CWC is compelling: relevant provisions establish U.S. responsibility retroactively, as far back as 1925. Each State Party must undertake to "destroy all chemical weapons it abandoned on the territory of another State Party . . ."[58] including all "chemical weapons, abandoned by a state after 1 January 1925 on the territory of another state without the consent of the latter."[59] Thus, all States Parties to the CWC bear the burden of retroactive responsibility for destroying chemical weapons left on the territory of another state, without its permission, dating back to 1925—some seventy-two years prior to the CWC Convention itself.

The CWC also establishes another retroactive date, pertaining to States Parties' obligations to destroy chemical weapon production and storage facilities that remain on foreign soil: "Chemical weapons production facility means any equipment, as well as any building housing such equipment that was designed, constructed or used at any time since 1 January 1946."[60]

The CWC clearly places responsibility on states reaching back decades, and yet this requirement has been largely ignored by the U.S. When the first cleanup efforts were undertaken in Vietnam, nearly a decade after the CWC was adopted, they were initiated not by the U.S. but by the Vietnamese government.

The strikingly limited U.S. response, and the unusually casual manner in which cleanup was addressed, represent more than a thumbing of the nose at international law. This signifies a flagrant disregard by a major world power for the long-term and systemic damage that U.S. chemical weapons cause among those who come into direct or indirect contact with them.

But there is a much more searing—and ever-present—threat, discussed in Chapter 3: Agent Orange-related exposure may still be impacting the very gene pool of the Vietnamese people.

The U.S. Congress itself gave a significant nod to the recognition of the threat of dioxin to human health when it established a program of funding and support for its own Vietnam War veterans who had been exposed to dioxin. The same, however, was never considered or done for Vietnamese families who continue to suffer from dioxin exposure.

In short, the United States has never acknowledged its responsibility for the continuing illnesses and deaths among Vietnamese civilians related to Agent Orange exposure, nor has it contemplated what, if any, responsibility it bears for reparations to these innocent victims.

CHAPTER FIVE

The U.S. and Customary World Standards

By the mere fact of having sent [its planes to] a foreign country...
and in doing so having caused damage and destruction contrary to
Humanitarian Law, whatever the modus operandi, constitutes an
illegal act by which the United States has made itself responsible
for the consequences and is obligated to rectify them.

PUBLIC APPEAL OF INTERNATIONAL LAWYERS CONCERNING
THE RESPONSIBILITY OF THE UNITED STATES TOWARD VIETNAM,
FRANCIS BOYLE, ET AL., *April 29, 2007*

The international treaties and conventions we have just
analyzed—along with many others—are part of a broader
but related legal framework that dates back several centuries.
This framework is known as *customary international law* (CIL).
Although independent of treaty law per se, CIL evolved from
the shared practices and obligations typically accepted by
states. Treaties and conventions pertain to specific expectations
and rules of conduct governing issues such as the treatment
of women, ethnic and religious minorities, or civilians in
wartime. Customary international law, on the other hand, is

more comprehensive. It encompasses practices that in some instances are considered preemptory international norms from which no state may derogate irrespective of treaty law itself.

As a legally established international framework, CIL is recognized in the Charter of the United Nations, the Statute of the International Court of Justice (ICJ)—the principal judicial organ of the United Nations—and by nations and institutions worldwide.[1] Not only do the Charter and the Statute both recognize CIL, they also note that upholding it is the key responsibility of the ICJ: to "decide in accordance with international law [and] apply . . . international custom, as evidence of a general practice accepted as law."[2] CIL must meet two components: a general and consistent practice of states, and a sense of legal obligation of states that they are bound to it (*opinio juris*).[3] A practice, therefore, does not become a rule of customary law simply because it is widely followed; rather, states must consider it obligatory as a matter of law.[4] As such, a rule or principle that is reflected in the conduct of states must be accepted by states expressly or tacitly as legally binding internationally.[5]

If, on the other hand, a given practice is followed merely out of courtesy, or if states believe they are legally free to depart from it, CIL cannot be upheld.[6] At the same time, many jurists and legal scholars hold that a practice need not be universally followed, but must nevertheless have obtained general acceptance to be considered customary international law.[7]

In fact, some scholars distinguish CIL from treaty law in that CIL is "pervasive enough internationally that countries need not consent to be bound [by it]."[8] Whereas treaty law is binding only to States Parties, when a norm is established as customary international law it becomes binding on all states[9] and can be used to fill in gaps or complement treaty law.[10] In this sense, CIL extends the reach of the rules to states that have not yet ratified [a] treaty;[11] this reach is thus considered to possess more jurisprudential power than treaty law itself.[12] This is illustrated, according to international law professor Michael Sharf, by the principle that "the customary international law status of the rules can apply to actions of treaty parties that <u>predated the entry into force</u> of the treaty."[13] (Emphasis added).

The above notwithstanding, it is often difficult to determine when a state practice meets the threshold of customary international law.[14] Even if a practice has been followed on a widespread basis, and out of a sense of obligation on the part of states, it remains somewhat unclear how widely accepted a practice must be to meet the test.[15]

CIL: A Brief History

Customary law has been recognized as a concept central to jurisprudence dating back to the mid-seventeenth century. While international law is often considered to have emerged in Europe after the Peace of Westphalia in 1648, evidence indicates that the practice of customary law was not unique to Europe, but in fact shared by many cultures and societies—the Near East, Greece, Rome, China, Islam, and "Western Christendom"—whose coexistence largely depended upon the establishment of shared rules and norms in peace and in war.[16] These societies practiced tacit consent, which was due not to a contractual agreement but to tradition, something quite similar to contemporary practices of social customs.[17] As such, in the Middle Ages, custom was not clearly defined but existed as an indeterminate set of possible conforming behaviors.[18] However, ambiguity about the threshold of time required in order for a practice to be considered customary has generated debate among jurists that continues to this day.

As the practice of customary law developed over time, its definition and application grew more tangible and was reflected in law codified after World War II, including in the Statute of the International Court of Justice. This formal recognition of customary law was emblematic of developing law at the time, including an increase in the number of international conventions and treaties.

Over the past hundred years or so, three instruments have played a particularly strong role in the development of customary international law—The Hague Conventions, The Treaty of Versailles, and the Geneva Conventions—because of their treatment of armed conflict and their contributions to global legal standards. As such, these instruments exemplify two of the primary elements of modern international law, namely the rules of conduct during armed conflict and protections for civilians. The former is often referred as to "Hague law" and the latter as "Geneva law," reflecting their geographic origins.

The Hague Conventions of 1899 and 1907 govern the use of weapons against civilian populations, prohibit the employment of arms that can cause superfluous injury, and prohibit attacks on areas that are not defended. They also require an occupying power to take all steps to re-establish and ensure public order and safety,[19] and prohibit the suffering or deaths of civilians. Notably, the Conventions introduce two specific requirements: the obligation of belligerent parties to be responsible for acts committed by persons in its armed forces, and for those parties to pay compensation for any violation of the Conventions' provisions.

The relevance and importance of The Hague Conventions regarding the laws of war is noted by the International Committee of the Red Cross, namely that "the provisions of the two Conventions on land warfare, like most of the substantive provisions of The Hague Conventions of 1899 and 1907, are considered as embodying rules of customary international law. As such, they are also binding on states which are not formally parties to them."[20] The Conventions marked an advance over extant international law at the time of their adoption and they were recognized by civilized states as being declaratory of the laws and customs of war as early as 1939.[21]

The Treaty of Versailles in 1919 concluded World War I by instituting an accord between Germany and the Allied

Powers that established guidelines for continued peace. It required Germany to disarm and also to make concessions and pay reparations to certain states. Article 231 of the Treaty required Germany to "accept the responsibility of [herself] and her allies for causing the loss and damage to which the Allied and Associated Governments and their nationals have been subjected . . ."[22] while Article 232 obligated Germany to "make compensation for all damage done to the civilian population of the Allied and Associated Powers and to their property during the period of the belligerency [including] aggression by land, by sea and from the air . . ."[23] In addition to compensatory measures, Germany was also required to make reimbursement,[24] as determined by the Reparation Commission.

It is notable that contemporary legal analysts and human rights observers consider the Treaty to have been an overly punitive instrument and one that likely led Germany to World War II. At minimum, the post-war reparations then imposed on Germany are no longer the types of reparations typically imposed under current international law. While analysts differ on the importance of the Treaty with respect to the application of reparations, the topic is addressed here because of its historic importance and because it is a major thread in the development of the concept and practice of reparations within the international community.

The Geneva Conventions of 1949 were developed in the aftermath of World War II as a step towards mitigating the barbarity of war and establishing stronger civilian protections during armed conflict. The idea for the four conventions was conceived at a diplomatic conference in Geneva to discuss international humanitarian law in the wake of World War II. Convention IV, the one of greatest relevance to the protection of civilians during war, states that civilians shall be treated humanely and protected against threats and acts of violence, and it places responsibility on respective warring parties for said treatment. It also prohibits States Parties from taking any measure that could cause the suffering or deaths of protected persons such as civilians. The first of the Conventions' three Additional Protocols offers similar protections for civilians, prohibiting indiscriminate attacks as defined within the text, and requiring parties to the conflict to avoid placing military objects near or in densely populated areas.

The historical contributions of these agreements to the development of customary international law stand alongside numerous others governing the norms and behavior of states. Appendix B provides a listing of many such instruments. In some instances, embodied in the concept of *jus cogens*, customary international law requires states to operate in accordance with global norms that may exist independent of individual treaties. With respect to torture, genocide, and slavery, for example, states may not derogate from established norms, and neither can they legally hold that nuances of treaties absolve them of adherence to these global standards of customary law.[25] While such *jus cogens* norms do not cover obligations for post-war cleanup and reparations for civilians harmed or killed by ordnance and chemical weapons, we can consider whether the U.S. failed to follow customary world standards by using weapons such as cluster bombs and Agent Orange, particularly against civilian populations.

While some might argue that the Vietnam War is long over and the types of weapons used at the time are now irrelevant to the above consideration of international law, such an argument would have to overcome a triple hurdle:

- If the weapons used were illegal under customary international law at the time of the War, their deployment would have been in violation of CIL irrespective of the passage of time;
- If weapons were used against civilian populations, their deployment would have been in violation of both treaty and customary international law; and, most importantly,
- If U.S. weapons continue to maim and kill Vietnamese civilians even today, the argument of their irrelevance due to the passage of time is turned on its head, rendering the U.S. *currently* in violation of customary international law.

At the outset of these considerations, it is important to note that the United States itself recognizes the concept and application of customary international law. Among many assents to CIL, the U.S. signed the Vienna Convention on the Law of

Treaties in 1970, noting that it "considers many provisions of the Convention to constitute customary international law on the law of treaties," and recognizes it as binding.[26] Moreover, in both diplomatic writings and international forums the United States has consistently referenced customary law as an existing and binding concept of international jurisprudence. The international community, for example, has condemned the use of chemical weapons for nearly a hundred years, and continues to do so today, as evidenced by backlash to their use by the Assad regime in Syria. And the 1925 Geneva Protocol, as we have seen, held that chemical weapons are never to be used "under any circumstances." This general prohibition, now widely accepted as a shared international norm, has been woven into more recent treaty law, notably in the Chemical Weapons Convention discussed in the previous chapter.

Moreover, two resolutions passed by the United Nations General Assembly also elucidate the relevance of CIL in the matter of U.S. cleanup responsibility. In 1966, without any dissent, the General Assembly passed Resolution 2162B, which called for all states to observe the 1925 Geneva Protocol prohibiting the use of poisonous gases.[27] Three years later, the General Assembly passed another resolution declaring that the prohibition of chemical and biological weapons in international armed conflicts, as embodied in the 1925 Protocol, is a generally recognized rule of international law.[28] This prohibition is now widely accepted [and] considered as customary international law, binding even on states that have not joined the Protocol.[29]

As for the use of explosive devices in Vietnam, particularly cluster bombs, it is less clear that customary international law prohibits their use. It is the nature of war, after all, that a variety of explosive devices are used by combatants against one another. But cluster bombs have been singled out as particularly reprehensible because of their ability to kill or maim many people at a time, including innocent civilians. The world community took a step toward rendering the use of cluster bombs illegal as an international norm through the adoption of the Convention on Cluster Munitions, even though the U.S. refused to sign it. Clearly one convention alone, particularly a relatively recent one, does not transform a standard into customary law.

The question remains, however, whether the U.S. or any other nation may feel free to ignore *developing* customary international law. If, for example, the prohibition against cluster bombs is now accepted by a majority of states worldwide, a prohibition the U.S. itself accepts in most instances, what can be the justification for leaving bombs on Vietnamese soil that continue to kill people today? Is the apparent double standard of professing to accept the prohibition of cluster bombs while leaving the very same bombs active on the soil of another country somehow justified under treaty law or international law? We shall re-visit this issue in the next chapter.

Customary Law and the U.S. in Vietnam
The weight of the evidence thus far solidly suggests that it is prohibited for any nation to knowingly wage war against

civilians. The Hague Conventions of 1899 and 1907, which address the conduct of war including the protection of civilians, were standards so clear and transformative that they were later incorporated into the military codes of various nations including the United States. Similarly, Hague Convention II on Laws and Customs of War on Land further prohibits the wounding or killing of civilians, including military attacks against undefended areas. The Geneva Conventions of 1949 also mitigate the barbarity of war by establishing protections for civilians from the threat or actual experience of war-related violence. Convention provisions prohibit indiscriminate attacks and military missions from being carried out near or within densely populated areas.

With the aforementioned conventions establishing both widely held obligations and long-accepted international practices to protect civilians during times of war, and other, more recent conventions and international discourse among nations reflecting the same standards, it can hardly be denied that the practice of not harming civilian populations during war time is part of customary international law. It is in this context that U.S. actions in Vietnam may be evaluated. Were civilians impacted? If so, how? Was the impact accidental or intentional, minimal or major? And was said impact short-lived or more sustained and large-scale?

That numerous Vietnamese civilians were killed and maimed during the War is uncontested. While estimates of the exact figure vary, as discussed in Chapters 2 and 3, U.S. military records, Vietnamese government records, and those of international entities place the numbers in the hundreds of thousands if not millions. Moreover, as noted in Dr. Jeanne Stellman's report to Congress (Chapter 3), the number of "silent" victims of the War due to Agent Orange exposure alone was 4,800,000, and this number does not even include the millions poisoned later due to the introduction of dioxin into the food chain.[30]

When this impact is combined with the number of civilians maimed or killed by U.S. cluster bombs—during the War and to this day—little question exists but that U.S. military operations violated standards of customary international law. That the impact on civilians was not simply incidental or mistaken is reflected not only in the magnitude of the numbers just mentioned, but also in the widespread use of cluster bombs and Agent Orange by the United States. Some 43% of cultivated land was poisoned; 60% of plantations; and 36% of forested land. More than 6,000 square kilometers of land in southern Vietnam alone remain unsuitable for agriculture, and their water sources were polluted on a massive scale.[31]

In light of U.S. use of weapons prohibited under both treaty law and customary law, and particularly in light of their use against innocent civilians on a widespread and sustained basis, we may now ask, what obligations does customary law place on the U.S. with respect to post-war cleanup? Framing the question more broadly, what responsibilities do combatant countries have for removing or destroying weapons left on the land of other states, particularly when they constitute an ongoing threat to civilian populations?

Little question exists that post-war cleanup is required as a matter of customary international law, particularly given the development of treaty law over recent decades, highlighting the responsibility of warring parties to clean up the weapons they leave behind.[32] Cleanup responsibility also has been consistently stressed in other international forums, such as the United Nations Human Rights Committee and the European Court of Human Rights. Furthermore, responsibility for post-war cleanup has never been contested by the United States as a matter of record. In fact, by signing the 1973 Paris Peace Accords that ended its involvement in Vietnam, the United States declared that it would "contribute to erase the wounds of the War and to the post-war reconstruction of the Democratic Republic of Vietnam."[33] It would be virtually inconceivable to suggest that this commitment, particularly in light of existing treaty law at the time, would not cover removal of live ordnance and dioxin.

With responsibility for cleanup ignored for decades by the United States, and given its significantly limited and highly tardy response in addressing Agent Orange exposure in Vietnam, a final consideration regarding the relevance of customary international law concerns U.S. responsibility for reparations to innocent civilian victims.

According to the International Center for Transitional Justice, reparations are an established practice of acknowledging the legal obligation of a state or entity to "repair the consequence of violations, either because it directly committed them or it failed to prevent them."[34] As such, reparations are considered to be the most direct and meaningful way of delivering justice.[35] The practice is recognized in both treaty law and customary international law, and is a frequent practice of states worldwide to make amends for wrongdoing.

The right to reparations on the one hand, and the duty to provide them on the other, constitute a principle of law that has existed for centuries.[36] It is recognized and secured by the United Nations,[37] in myriad human rights and humanitarian treaties,[38] in legal instruments,[39] and also in customary international law, as noted. It is a principle of customary law that the breach of an engagement involves an obligation to make reparations in an adequate form,[40] and as such, reparations must, as far as possible, wipe out all the consequences of the illegal act and re-establish the situation which would, in all probability, have existed if that act had not been committed.[41]

Since the time Germany was required to make reparations for damage caused during World War I, international concern about the aftermath of armed conflict has increased substantially,[42] with the psychosocial impacts of World War II adding to the magnitude of violence against civilian victims. The practice of reparations now extends beyond wartime damages alone to include compensatory and other measures for individuals and groups for severe human rights violations.[43] While much of the attention on civilian harm has focused on unlawful activities, recent legal arguments and state practices point to the development of a framework for assisting civilians harmed by both lawful and unlawful conduct during combat.[44] International law now recognizes several forms of reparations including restitution, compensation, rehabilitation and the guarantee of non-repetition.[45]

Because the state is the first line of defense in human rights law, with the obligation to respect, protect, and fulfill rights,[46] a state that violates international humanitarian law must make full reparation for losses and injuries.[47] So preeminent is this notion that it is considered to be applicable in both international and non-international armed conflicts.[48]

This norm was manifest in the 1928 ruling of the Chorzow Factory case made by the Permanent Court of International Justice—now the International Court of Justice—which stated that "it is a principle of international law, and even a general conception of the law, that any breach of an engagement involves an obligation to make reparation . . . and *there is no necessity for this to be stated in the convention itself.*"[49] (Emphasis added.) This ruling indicates that in addition to being secured in treaty law, reparations also are recognized as a normative measure—in other words an accepted and essential component of customary international law.

The actual practice of reparations did not begin with the Treaty of Versailles, nor did it end there. It includes the descendants of individuals enslaved during the Atlantic slave trade, as called for by the African Repatriation Truth Commission; reparations for aboriginal Canadian families whose children were placed in church-run schools in an effort to homogenize Canada; and reparations for families of the disappeared in Chile under the regime of Agosto Pinochet. In the latter case, families were awarded monthly pensions, access to a specialized health care program, exemption from military service, and educational benefits for children.[50]

The right to reparations is also recognized and practiced by the United States:

1. Forty years after the internment of 60,000 Japanese-Americans during World War II, the U.S. government provided reparations for survivors including an official apology, establishment of a trust fund, and the provision of direct monetary payments.[51]

2. The U.S. made reparations to Afghani civilians under the Afghan Civilian Assistance Program for those harmed by the presence of the international military.[52]

3. It provided reparations through the Iraqi War Victims Fund to families suffering losses resulting from U.S. military operations since 2003.[53]

4. It paid reparations to Switzerland for the accidental bombing of the town of Schaffhausen during World War II.

5. In the 1950s it paid financial compensation to Japan after conducting an atomic bomb test in the Pacific that exposed a Japanese fishing boat and its crew to radiation.[54]

In short, the United States is quite familiar with the principle and practice of reparations. With regard to Vietnam, after some years of averring responsibility for compensation to its own Vietnam veterans, the U.S. changed its policy due to Congressional pressure and now provides compensation to military personnel who had been exposed to Agent Orange.[55] In terms of reparations for the ongoing harm inflicted upon individual Vietnamese civilians, however, none have been offered or provided by the United States.

It would be most difficult to establish a sustainable justification to support the U.S. government's decision to compensate its own veterans while never compensating—let alone recognizing—the impact of the same harm to innocent Vietnamese civilians. While the Geneva Conventions of 1949 did distinguish between obligations to one's own civilians and obligations to the enemy, obligations to both are noted. But in the current context Vietnamese civilians are not the enemy but civilians, and arguably no different than the Afghani or Iraqi civilians to whom the U.S. has provided reparations for damages from its military operations in 2003. Moreover, the principle of reparations suggests that a state is responsible for providing reparations to all of the victims of its transgressions who have suffered in a similar manner.

To summarize, reparations are an established principle of customary international law, and the responsibility to provide them is considered so clear that it need not be noted in individual conventions.[56] It would therefore be in accordance with international standards for the United States to provide reparations to Vietnamese civilians for the ongoing harm caused by excessive exposure to Agent Orange as well as the continuing explosions of left-behind ordnance.

It is difficult to discern whether the long silence of the U.S. is simply a strategic avoidance of the issues or if some rationale supports its inaction. It is possible that the U.S. might advance two legal arguments to seek to justify the failure to act. One is that relevant treaties governing weapons of war and the targeting of civilians did not exist at the time of the Vietnam War, and the other is that international obligations governing post-war cleanup and reparations are not retroactive in nature and, thus, place no burden on the U.S. to act.

However, both arguments fail to withstand scrutiny. Long before the United States entered Vietnam, both treaty law and customary international law banned the use of chemical weapons as acceptable agents in times of armed conflict. Moreover, the prohibition on targeting innocent civilians had long been established as an international standard—largely established by the Hague and Geneva Conventions—and one that certainly existed at the time the U.S. targeted Vietnamese civilians with explosive and chemical weapons on a sustained basis. The weight of international law, in both relevant treaties and customary law, does not permit the United States to claim that its departure from Vietnam obviates its legal responsibility for the types of weapons it used, or for using them against civilian populations.

As noted, post-war obligations for cleanup, as well as the destruction of abandoned weapons of war, extend back to the Geneva Protocol of 1925. The more recent Chemical Weapons Convention places the burden for cleanup on states retroactively to 1946. In addition, extant treaty law places responsibility for cleanup on states even if they had left behind weapons prior to the relevant legal instrument, a requirement pertaining not only to chemical weapons but also to explosive ordnance.[57]

Similarly, it is an unassailable position that cleanup is a necessary component of any weapons ban. For states to be held accountable for abolishing weapons post-war, but then to be permitted to let them remain on the ground, would undermine the very purpose of cleanup. The fundamental reason for post-war cleanup, after all, is to protect civilians who may be harmed or even killed by weapons after hostilities have ended. The logic of this is rendered even more poignant in the case of Vietnam.

Finally, let us re-visit the argument for reparations to Vietnamese civilians maimed or killed by the United States. While the U.S. has ignored the subject altogether, it would not be possible to sustain an argument for exemption from such responsibility on the basis of timing or retroactivity. The concept and practice of reparations arose long before U.S. entry into Vietnam, and reparations are, by their very nature, *ex post facto*.

In light of both treaty law and customary international law, the overwhelming evidence is that the United States violated international laws of war with the types of weapons it deployed in Vietnam and with their indiscriminate use against civilians. And in the forty years following the end of the War, the U.S. has violated its obligations to remove its live weapons from Vietnamese soil, or even to consider reparations responsibilities to Vietnamese families maimed and killed by its actions both during and after the War.

CHAPTER SIX

Rule of Law or Scofflaw

> There will be justice in Athens when those who are
> not injured are as outraged as those who are.
>
> THUCYDIDES

Four decades have passed since the end of the Vietnam War. We will soon approach 50 years since the last American troops departed the small Southeast Asian nation. Official counts indicate that during the years of U.S. involvement, the conflict resulted in the deaths of up to 1.4 million American and Vietnamese troops combined, and some 400,000 civilian victims, as noted in Chapter 1. But the War has yet to end for Vietnamese families. The intervening decades have been marked by the injuries and deaths of at least 100,000 more Vietnamese children and adults from explosive ordnance left behind by U.S. troops. Yet this is but one type of toll. America's widespread spraying of poisonous defoliants on farms, rice paddies, and villages constitutes another component of the "continuing war," particularly for generations of Vietnamese children born after the end of formal hostilities.

It is difficult to fathom how a war that has ended can continue on with grievous harm to civilians long after armed conflict is over. We might, in fact, ask how a war could possibly be considered over when the deaths of innocent civilians continue for decades.

Generations ago, states had few remedies by which to address the continuing costs of war, particularly for civilians, nor did they readily have meaningful avenues by which to assess and assign responsibility for the ongoing harm that resulted. Even well into the 20th century, the world had few meaningful ways to address the debilitating impact of wars' aftermath.

The situation is not the same today. The world now has a robust body of international law that governs the types of weapons used by combatants, the responsibilities of states for post-war cleanup and reparations, and even the assignment of possible criminal responsibility to state and military leaders who fail to comply with shared standards. No longer are violations of accepted standards of conduct simply the "tough luck" of civilians who suffer the life-threatening brunt of unbridled military aggression. No longer are nations and citizens of the world left without a response other than the feeling of miserable helplessness. International law requires states to adhere to shared standards of responsibility and can place constraints, restrictions and rebuke on those that do not comply.

But if this legal framework that the world now shares is to bear any meaningful significance in the relationships and conduct of states, particularly with respect to safeguarding the lives of citizens, states must honor not only the letter of the law but also the general principles of developing humanitarian standards. This is particularly important for large and powerful nations such as the United States that claim world leadership, promote enlightened approaches to governance, and espouse adherence to the rule of law.

It is in this context that we now review U.S. responsibility for the weapons of war it used and left in Vietnam nearly 50 years ago. What does international law require regarding the weapons used by the United States? What responsibility does the United States bear for cleaning up the weapons it left in Vietnam that continue to threaten the lives of women, men, and children? What does international law suggest regarding U.S. responsibility for the lives of the 100,000 Vietnamese civilians maimed or killed since American troops left the country, as well as generations of children deformed by DNA alterations passed down from their parents and grandparents who suffered Agent Orange exposure? And finally, what pressures and entities can help enforce international law?

Discussion of the various international conventions in preceding chapters, nested within the framework of customary international law, supports the conclusions that the United States:

- Used military weapons in Vietnam that had been outlawed decades earlier, particularly poisonous chemical agents;
- Deployed weapons in Vietnam, including cluster bombs and Agent Orange, that are illegal under today's existing international standards;
- Used both chemicals and cluster bombs on a widespread basis against innocent civilians;
- Has never officially acknowledged that its weapons are still maiming and killing Vietnamese people and that, therefore, its war-related hostilities continue even today;
- Has failed to accept full responsibility for cleaning up the unexploded ordnance it left on Vietnamese soil; and
- Has never addressed or officially considered any responsibility for reparations to Vietnamese civilians killed by left-behind live ordnance or poisoned by Agent Orange, even though it has reluctantly acknowledged the impact of this poisonous chemical on its own troops and awarded reparatory stipends to American veterans.

Given the relevance of current international law to the role of the U.S. during the Vietnam War, how might we understand America's failure to acknowledge and fully consider its post-war responsibility to the Vietnamese people? Perhaps the only explanation is that the United States sometimes considers international law an elective rather than a mandatory legal obligation. Like many other nations, the United States has viewed treaty provisions to which it is bound as mere expectations from which it is free to exempt itself.

On some occasions it has refused even the expansion of international law. To date, for example, the United States has not agreed to the complete ban of cluster bombs. Along with a small handful of nations including Russia, Pakistan, China, and Israel, the U.S. has refused to join the 100+ nations who now hold the use of cluster bombs to be an inhumane and unacceptable practice.

Since the American government exempts itself from this generally accepted international standard, does that suggest that it is legally exempt and thus has an absolute right to employ cluster bombs against other nations? Does that mean, in turn, that it is acceptable for the U.S. to disregard international standards when it simply elects to do so? And if the answer to either or both questions is in the affirmative, what does this suggest about America's claim to world leadership and its avowed respect for the rule of law?

By exercising the privilege of unilateral action, the U.S. benefits from conflicting choices: seeking acceptance and recognition as a world leader in the international community while reserving the wiggle room to ignore established legal norms, when deemed convenient. But in failing to recognize and comply with certain treaties, circumscribing key elements of treaties it otherwise recognizes, and quibbling over the language of others, the U.S. government undermines its standing as a world leader.

The U.S. cannot justifiably argue that it's unaware of the ordnance and chemicals it left behind. Nor can it claim ignorance of the deaths its chemical agents and munitions continue to cause among the civilian population of Vietnam. Because this knowledge is part of the international public record, such arguments would be considered fanciful at best. Neither could the U.S. sustain a logical argument that it lacks responsibility due to the thin thread of timing, namely that some relevant treaties which apply now were not in force at the time of the War. Such a position would be a fool's errand since America's unexploded weapons are still at work today, making any and all of these existing treaty provisions relevant today, irrespective of their dates of adoption. Any U.S. weapons and actions that may not have been illegal under international law at the time of the Vietnam War are illegal now, since the U.S. is allowing them to kill Vietnamese people today.

The weight of the evidence—the body of conventions established and employed over decades, customary international law, and the practices of state and international institutions— strongly indicates that regardless of any ambiguity in specific treaty provisions, it is in both the spirit and developing trajectory of international law for the U.S. to facilitate the removal and destruction of explosive remnants of war in Vietnam, make the country and its people safe from dioxin poisoning related to Agent Orange, and provide appropriate reparations for victims and families harmed inter-generationally by the spraying of poisonous chemicals on their forests, fields and rivers.

Given these considerations, the U.S. appears to have no logical or meaningful reprieve from responsibility under international law. This leaves the U.S. with several options:

OPTION ONE: It could simply continue to ignore its responsibilities regarding Vietnam. This type of let-sleeping-dogs-lie approach would certainly free the U.S. from addressing such a thorny issue and possibly bring along the financial benefits of not having to provide reparations. But America's continued silence could weaken the efficacy of international law, undermine U.S. claims to world leadership with respect to human rights, and almost certainly lead to the continued maiming and killing of innocent Vietnamese civilians. It could even embolden other nations to disregard international law in a similar manner.

OPTION TWO: A second and much more desirable option, and one where all parties would benefit, would be for the U.S. to materially acknowledge the compelling issues of explosive ordnance and Agent Orange exposure, including the obligation to initiate cleanup and reparations. One way to do this effectively would be to work with the Vietnamese government to remove and destroy the ordnance, and propose additional Congressional funding for cleanup of all toxic hotspots.

Formal acknowledgement and action steps would provide Vietnamese families with at least some closure, and doing so publicly would provide greater meaning than doing so privately. This option could also permit the global community to reevaluate its commitments to international law and help ensure the physical safety of communities impacted by war.

OPTION THREE: A third option would be that relevant Congressional committees hold hearings to better understand the nature and dimensions of the problem of left-behind ordnance, help educate the public about it as well, and consider appropriate steps to take under international law. These hearings could be conducted in one of two ways: holding either an investigation to scrutinize the responsibility of the U.S. government, or legislative hearings to formulate steps to provide fully for cleanup and reparations. Hearings would likely garner greater exposure about the issue of post-war harm to civilians and help to limit future situations.

OPTION FOUR: A final option is that the international community itself—possibly through the United Nations or even a quasi-independent, multilateral international body—investigate U.S. conduct under existing law, and point to areas of responsibility that have not yet been formally recognized by the U.S.

As is evident with the case of the U.S. in Vietnam, increasing state compliance with obligations under international law requires much more than the goodwill and the legal commitments of states. Pressure from the international community by way of global institutions, non-governmental organizations and other nations, in combination, are required to enforce compliance. The international community must apply the same unwavering insistence to impose compliance with legal obligations of post-war cleanup and reparations that it applies to other laws of war.

––––––––

Formal United States participation in the Vietnam War ended when its troops departed the country in the early 1970s, but the War has yet to end. Deaths continue to accrue from ordnance explosions and from congenital diseases associated with Agent Orange exposure. They will continue to mount indefinitely unless the United States takes appropriate steps.

Little else seems to exemplify the gravity of continued post-war suffering as much as the fact that this matter is not unique to Vietnam and that it impacts nations across the globe. Ongoing post-war violence is not limited to a particular country or region; it's an outcome experienced by many who have been impacted by war. According to the International Committee of the Red Cross, ordnance remain in other post-conflict regions including Bosnia and Herzegovina, Iraq, Rwanda, Nicaragua, and Sri Lanka, among others. If the United States were to take meaningful and appropriate steps in Vietnam, it would no doubt open the door for the accountability of other states for removing the explosive remnants of other wars. Yet much still remains contingent upon the U.S. formally recognizing and accepting its responsibility.

With respect to Vietnam, America has two notable choices: to demonstrate respect for the rule of law, or to shirk it by remaining an international scofflaw.

CHAPTER SEVEN

Strengthening the Arms of Justice

> I am going to ask member states, "Are the crimes not serious enough for you to investigate? Do you think that there is no evidence for you to collect?"
>
> AMAL ALAMUDDIN CLOONEY
> *International Human Rights Lawyer,*
> *Columbia University*

We now consider the United States' role in Vietnam in the broader context of state behavior within the international community. For many nations, the promise of human rights protections remains stronger than the reality on the ground. Scofflaw behavior—ignoring or flouting the law—is not unique to the U.S.; strengthening adherence to international law is required to reduce opportunities for states to ignore or evade international standards.

This may come as little surprise. After all, if the U.S.— with its economic capacity, world standing and long-avowed commitment to the rule of law—has difficulty complying with human rights treaty obligations, states with less economic power and capacity would likely have similar problems. But this argument, even if accurate, is too simplistic. The failure of so many states to comply often has less to do with their actual capacity than with raw politics. Their actions are driven by shrewd assessments of whether compliance is in the interest of the state, specifically those in power. What is to be gained by compliance? What is to be lost if we don't comply? Will internal adversaries—competing political parties, religious factions, public opinion—oppose compliance or support it? In short, the perceived self-interest of states often supersedes the efficacy of international law.

The simple truth is that many nations assess and protect their internal political interests first, and treat their compliance with international law as a secondary priority. Analogous to U.S. ordnance in Vietnam, for example, is the unexploded ordnance that remain in Bosnia from the attacks on Bosnian Muslims during that conflict, ordnance in Mozambique from its fifteen-year war, and numerous others. According to the 2016 *Landmine and Cluster Munition Monitor,* which assesses compliance with the 1977 Mine Ban Treaty, more than 60 states continue to be impacted by anti-personnel mines.[1] Many countries flout still other areas of international law: dictator Augusto Pinochet of Chile ordered the disappearance, torture and murder of thousands who opposed his regime; the Hutu-led forces of the Rwandan government perpetrated the genocide of Tutsis; the government in Darfur conducted a campaign of ethnic cleansing against its non-Arab citizens;

Bashar al-Assad of Syria stands in violation of international law by the gassing of his own citizenry; and the government of Myanmar has driven out large numbers of its Rohingya population through state-sanctioned violence. These examples stand out in the public mind, largely due to the combination of the atrocities committed and the related media attention, but they are simply emblematic of a larger number of human rights violations throughout the world.

But let us begin with the good news. Over the past seventy years or more, the global community has created a comprehensive body of treaty law reflecting shared human rights standards, and has worked to increase state accountability through enforcement bodies and mechanisms such as the United Nations. Establishing this legal framework has been a long and arduous process, one that is ongoing to be sure, yet there is no doubt that it has improved the lives of countless people around the globe. Many of the states that have ratified international treaties have taken meaningful steps to comply, such as making primary education compulsory and free for all children; providing equal employment opportunities for women and men; preventing and redressing the dispossession of indigenous peoples; addressing the health and educational needs of people with disabilities; and making progress in the still highly-contentious matter of the rights of refugees and immigrants.

But any informed observer would understand that these codifications of universal values, even in light of the tremendous progress made, are nowhere near sufficient to protect the legal rights of people worldwide. Daily news reports confirm that this is the case. The framework that has been created to protect human rights is only a start—a hope, even a promise—but not yet a meaningful guarantee of protection.

How States Undermine Treaty Law

The ways in which human rights treaties are undermined typically begin with the adoption of a treaty by states. The act of signing a treaty serves as an administrative pledge or intention by a government to comply with the treaty at some later date, but it is through ratification that a state formally commits to its obligations. For example, the U.S. may sign a treaty, but that treaty can only be ratified by the President with the consent of the Senate. States ambivalent about legally binding themselves to specific responsibilities often employ strategies to create enough wiggle room to avoid certain inconvenient or undesired obligations. They do so through the legally permitted process of expressing written *reservations*, language that effectively enables States Parties to avoid compliance with provisions they believe are incompatible with their perceived exigencies. In this sense, these states seek to have their cake and eat it too: ratification enables them to uphold their world standing as committed to safeguarding human rights, yet their stated reservations allow them some cover to avoid the external pressures experienced by states that have ratified the treaty without reservations.

A rather extreme example of how reservations can undermine the efficacy of a treaty can be found in the case of Saudi Arabia, in its ratification of the Convention on the Elimination of all Forms of Discrimination Against Women (CEDAW) in 2000. This was a notable treaty hailed around the world as a major achievement to overcome rampant gender inequality. It was particularly notable that CEDAW was adopted by Saudi Arabia and several other Arab states whose records on women's rights have often been the subject of international condemnation. But much of the world did not realize that Saudi Arabia was merely paying lip service to progressive compliance while it applied a number of formal reservations to avoid several provisions of the treaty. As noted by the United Nations, ". . . a general reservation [was] made by the State Party [Saudi Arabia] to the Convention whereby in case of a conflict between the provisions of Islamic law and those of the Convention, the State Party gives precedence to Islamic law."[2] In other words, Saudi Arabia only professed compliance with an international convention to which it was legally bound, but in the same breath reserved the right to ignore key provisions—at its own discretion. Saudi Arabia arguably had little intention of improving or strengthening its human rights practices and treatment of women, its ratification being a self-serving promise. Just as Saudi Arabia succumbed to cultural and religious pressures to cherry-pick the commitments to which it will adhere, other countries sometimes do the same.

The United States utilized a similar tactic when it ratified the Convention Against Torture (CAT) in 1994. It applied reservations to several articles, including Article 16, which prohibits cruel, inhuman or degrading treatment or punishment "in any territory under its jurisdiction." The United States' reservations were made on the grounds that it "considers itself bound to prevent cruel, inhuman or degrading treatment or punishment"[3] only to the extent that such treatment is prohibited "by the Fifth, Eighth, and/or Fourteenth Amendments to the Constitution of the United States."[4] This effectively allows the United States to reap the benefits of being a State Party[5] while ignoring provisions in its discretionary judgment.

While applying reservations is legally permitted under international law, states often use reservations to avoid full compliance with key provisions of treaties. Under the Vienna Convention on the Law of Treaties—which the U.S. considers part of CIL even though it has not ratified the Convention[6]—reservations are not permitted if they are incompatible with the object and purpose of the treaty. In other words, reservations are within the rights of states so long as they don't undermine the essence of the treaty in question.

Reservations are a mixed bag. States are far more likely to sign treaties with reservations than not sign at all; therefore allowing reservations might increase the number of signatory states and, in turn, encourage greater overall compliance with international law over time. In this sense, it may be better to have states commit to international standards with reservations than not commit at all. This seemingly positive outcome, however, is not without a downside. The very ability of states to apply reservations may in fact undermine the efficacy of the overall legal framework, particularly when the reservations exceed the boundaries permitted under the Vienna Convention.

Another way in which state actions undermine the human rights framework is by ratifying treaties in full without reservations, and then largely ignoring its commitments. This ranges from intentional disregard of the law to unintentional actions—such as when states find enforcement of the treaties they've signed too difficult to carry out, be it due to internal cultural or religious mores and the exigencies of political forces. The United States, for example, signed the Convention on the Rights of the Child (CRC) and ratified both of the Convention's optional protocols six years after its entry into force in 1989. But the U.S. never ratified the Convention itself, and thus has no legal obligation to it, only to the protocols. As such, the only standards to which the international community might hold the U.S. accountable regarding children's rights is through the narrowly fashioned protocols—which address the involvement of children in armed conflict, and the sale of children, child prostitution, and child pornography, thereby allowing the U.S. to ignore the provisions provided under the treaty itself.

States also undermine the development of international law more indirectly by not complying with and implementing key provisions. While international law requires free public education for all children, for example, school uniform and textbook fees often make access to education out of the question for millions of children whose families live in poverty.

Thus, although the right to education is on the international law docket and even ratified as a pledge by many states, the right vanishes when states undermine it through such practices. Similarly, comprehensive health care is an established right under the International Covenant on Economic, Social and Cultural Rights (1976), but access to care remains unattainable for many people throughout the world, including millions in the United States.

These examples reflect *compliance gaps* in which states fall short of implementing treaties to which they are legally bound. Such behavior indicates that current monitoring and enforcement mechanisms are not sufficient to guarantee, let alone enforce, human rights across the globe. This is not to suggest that the United Nations has no enforcement and monitoring mechanisms—it does, and in fact is the primary enforcement and monitoring body in the world—but it demonstrates that they are woefully inadequate. And without stronger enforcement on the part of the international community, human rights often are left to the discretion of individual states. These realities— paying lip service to some but not all treaty provisions, ratifying treaties but failing to enforce key provisions, and holding high the banner of a new treaty but then ignoring what is not politically acceptable—are the soft underbelly of the otherwise promising body of international law so carefully fashioned over many decades.

The United Nations, founded in 1945 and currently comprised of 193 member states, is the most widely accepted platform for establishing, implementing, and monitoring adherence to human rights commitments. It is the fulcrum of international attention regarding human rights concerns around the world, the major avenue for discourse, and the principal entity for overseeing the progress of states through a series of monitoring and evaluation procedures and actions.

Each of the major international human rights treaties[7] has its own UN monitoring committee to oversee state compliance. These committees, referred to as *treaty bodies*, follow a three-step process:

- Review of mandatory progress reports submitted to the UN by States Parties
- Responsive recommendations to each state to improve adherence to respective conventions
- Receipt and review of complaints from groups or individuals regarding possible state violations of rights

In the event that States Parties do not adequately implement treaty obligations, the United Nations may apply various strategies to enable, persuade, and pressure the states into compliance. In addition to issuing public reports on States Parties' implementation, the UN also appoints special rapporteurs, individuals who provide two types of service:

1. Monitor state compliance with specific subject areas such as the right to adequate housing, food,

education, water and sanitation, as well as torture, violence against women, and the freedoms of indigenous people.

2. Provide recommendations and technical knowledge to guide states toward greater compliance.

This enables the UN to monitor, persuade and even expose recalcitrant states. But the fundamental weakness in this elaborate system is that it effectively has no meaningful authority or viable enforcement mechanism to compel states to comply. This is not to say that none of the above strategies work, but that when they do it is through the actions of monitoring, persuading, and exposing states rather than through the power of actual enforcement authority. The result is that compliance is left largely to the discretion of individual states; consequently, adherence to law is uneven and at times non-existent. One example of how committing to human rights obligations on paper does not translate to commitment in practice is Saudi Arabia's ratification of CEDAW, mentioned before. The treaty includes specific commitments to gender equality in education, yet school facilities for females remain fewer and inferior compared to those for males. In addition, class sizes for female students are larger, the teachers typically less qualified, and access to library resources is greatly limited in comparison to school facilities for male students. [8]

It is in this sense that the field of international human rights continues to grapple with the core issue of treaty compliance on the part of States Parties. This monumental challenge in the field of human rights will, at minimum, require three developments:

- Fashion actual enforcement roles for the United Nations with respect to States Parties;
- Build stronger involvement of international non-governmental organizations (NGOs) to monitor and advocate for state compliance; and perhaps most importantly
- Strengthen "bottom up" capacity of local and civil society organizations within and among states to hold their governments accountable for safeguarding human rights.

Vehicles for Strengthening State Compliance

Creating actual enforcement mechanisms at the UN level warrants substantially greater international attention. It will require a more vigorous global discussion about how to strengthen the role of the United Nations. In addition, the global community needs even greater UN oversight authority, something many if not most states will be reluctant to support. This will of course take time, because it will involve numerous parties representing myriad cultures and political systems.

Let us consider the way that states enforce *their own* laws. No state in the world has a body of law left to the whim of individuals. Failure to comply with local, state, or federal laws brings consequences: financial penalties, loss of rights, even imprisonment. This raises the question whether violations of international law should have similar consequences: should a recalcitrant state that flouts human rights obligations not be required to appear before a UN body with the authority and power to order compliance via the imposition of fines, loss of privileges, or sanctions? The potential downside of such an action, however, is that states may become more reticent to ratify treaties in the first place, or even remove themselves as signatories.

While greater enforcement power is the imposing elephant in the room that many states overlook or outright ignore, other less hefty means also exist. UN treaty bodies typically identify and evaluate states that fall short of their commitments, but the sizeable number of UN member states often makes it difficult for sufficient follow-up from these oversight bodies. With 193 member states to report on, treaty bodies tend to rely on written reports rather than on more measurable indicators of progress. This system can of course be strengthened. One option could be introducing new criteria for treaty body reports that states are required to file, particularly those that require more hard data on actual progress. Asking tougher questions could pull the curtain back on particular implementation methods, making it more difficult for states to provide embellished or vague answers.

Another way to build stronger UN enforcement mechanisms is to focus more time-sensitive attention on the implementation of treaty body reports to ensure that states are fully enacting recommended changes in policies. This could be accomplished through increased professional capacity, such as the appointment of additional special rapporteurs or ambassadors of respective UN subsidiary groups who have the authority to work closely with individual states and require frequent and detailed country reports on implementation. The point of strengthening the current system in this manner is to limit the number of months or even years that states can evade compliance, notwithstanding the risk of fewer states becoming signatories.

Yet another avenue to bring states into greater compliance would be for UN agencies to work more closely with non-governmental organizations (NGOs) in member states. NGOs on the ground possess unique knowledge and direct experience with government adherence to international law, and enhancing partnerships with them could substantially expand UN knowledge and improve its ability to foster greater compliance.

This brings us to the second point regarding the challenges facing the field of human rights. Complementing the role of the United Nations are international NGOs whose chief purpose is to facilitate, persuade, and pressure states into greater compliance with their human rights obligations. While there are numerous international NGOs, two of the more well-known are Human Rights Watch and Amnesty International. The roles they play and strategies they carry out range from cooperative efforts to move states toward greater compliance (education, empowerment, partnerships), to more adversarial roles toward states perceived to be recalcitrant (litigation and public reprimanding).[9]

The strategic roles of international NGOs typically reflect the perceived intentions, needs and abilities of states to strengthen their compliance with treaties. States with strong infrastructure and resources, for example, may require different strategic responses from NGOs than more economically or politically vulnerable nations. Other key considerations include whether the state is authoritarian or democratic, whether it practices centralized or decentralized rule, and whether statehood is strong or weak in nature.[10] Strategies for bringing states into greater compliance with international law are a matter of great debate in the field of human rights, and relevant scholarly research suggests that it will continue to require a combination of certain specific strategies, namely capacity-building, persuasion, incentives, and coercion.[11]

The theory behind capacity-building is that aid and guidance can at times help to bring states into compliance. This strategy is typically employed when UN entities and NGOs work with states that wish to uphold their legal obligations but face barriers of capacity or knowledge. As such, capacity-building often involves assisting states with strengthening their administrative infrastructure, and building or increasing greater internal understanding and support among its citizenry and relevant elites. Such initiatives may include training administrative bodies to implement and enforce the legal obligations of states; providing advice and guidance to states about what has worked in similar situations; promoting public awareness, understanding, and acceptance of treaty law through education and the media; and increasing legal and administrative capacity through state agencies and other avenues such as law enforcement and the judiciary system.

Capacity-building might also require financial wherewithal, as the implementation of rights often entails dedicated expenditures; even states with comparatively strong economies at times face burdens that necessitate internal planning and financial support. To meet these challenges, states establish partnerships and networks for consultation and initiatives based on the experience and insights of other states and relevant institutions. Such capacity-building initiatives are directed primarily at strengthening states that have fragile economies or underdeveloped government infrastructure, or that suffer internal strife or weak leadership.

Persuasion tactics, on the other hand, typically involve efforts by NGOs to convince states to achieve greater compliance on their own. Persuasion may be accompanied by incentives for taking positive action, or by disincentives for failing to comply. Persuasion frequently goes hand-in-hand with capacity-building and employing interactive strategies adopted by NGOs that leverage education and advocacy to move states into greater compliance with human rights obligations.

Coercion is yet another strategy to improve compliance. It is often employed through NGO reports designed to publicly reprimand non-compliant states and sometimes augmented by forceful political, economic, or legal tactics. Through annual and periodic treaty body reports, the UN or NGOs can pressure complacent or recalcitrant states into greater compliance by globally exposing their failure to uphold their human rights obligations. Typically, states prefer not to be portrayed or named as entities at the fringes of the global community; indeed, being the subject of international criticism might generate sufficient shame to incentivize a state toward greater compliance.

For nations such as North Korea, whose global reputations seem of little internal concern and against whom name-and-shame tactics have had little effect, political and financial pressure may be more effective tools. NGOs can propose boycotts against noncompliant nations, such as advising tourists to avoid travel to specific countries, or recommending that other states and the general public not purchase those countries' products and/or services.

In terms of legal force, litigation is a tool to press for compliance with human rights obligations, although employing it in the international arena can be cumbersome and woefully slow. Even so, it is considered by some scholars as "one of the best strategies available for creating home-grown pro-rights jurisprudence"[12] by bridging international standards and domestic jurisprudence to ensure greater compliance. This may well be the case if litigation is carried out internally within the state itself, rather than through other jurisprudential systems.

But like the UN, international NGOs also face the challenge of strengthening their impact. And like the UN, they occasionally fall into the role of long-term monitoring and reporting on state noncompliance. In a recent conversation with the author, John G. (Jack) Healey, the former executive director of Amnesty International USA, put it this way: "If you go to the dentist and learn you have a seriously infected tooth, do you want them to fix it or tell you to go home and they'll monitor it? We have far too much monitoring in human rights and far too little fixing."[13] Implementing fixes—meaning stronger and more effective advocacy teeth—remains a crucial next step for international nongovernmental organizations.

Developing a stronger role for the UN and for international NGOs represents two critical ways to improve state compliance with international law. But it is quite possible that a third avenue will have the greatest long-term effect in terms of compliance— not the top-down methods of the UN and international NGOs, but the bottom-up approach of internal capacity-building. The idea behind this concept is that over the long term, states will be more likely to fulfill their human rights obligations if they experience strong internal pressure to do so. Outside forces and pressures come and go over time, and can be dismissed much more easily (as we have seen with North Korea), but internal pressures can be longer-lasting, more persuasive, and stronger in nature—and therefore more influential.

Many analysts consider that the strategy with the most significant long-term pay-off is the development and strengthening of local and national human rights watchdog groups. Already, organizations like U.S.-based Just Associates (JASS) are working to build the capacity of women's organizations in a number of countries. Through education and training, monitoring, advocacy, protests, and litigation, such organizations are becoming a force to move their governments toward greater compliance with human rights. This is not an easy avenue, as it is fraught with perils nested within the unique cultural and political influences of individual states. In a number of states, for example, local organizations face brutal dictatorships, repressive regimes, and other regressive forces often driven by race, gender, and religious ideology. Still, over time, such impediments tend to weaken in the face of persistent internal advocacy and education.

Structural and political shortcomings in the enforcement of international treaty law are common, and even of staggering proportions—staggering because the lack of adequate enforcement results in the loss of fundamental human rights of hundreds of millions of people in the world. Often this loss drives people into lives of dire poverty, sexual, religious, and economic subjugation, illness, and, not infrequently, early death.

We have considered how easy it is for a powerful nation like the U.S. to ignore its responsibility to clean up its live weapons in Vietnam, even when Vietnamese people continue to be maimed and killed. Yet Vietnam is but one example of continuing violence against innocent civilians after formal combat ends.

The serious lack of teeth in the bold and promising framework of human rights created over the past several decades cannot be denied. Even as these words are written, people suffer misery and death because states continue to undermine their obligations to human rights. This weakness in human rights law—the contrast between high platitudes and low compliance—will continue unless the international community acknowledges this problem and commits to stronger and more sufficient enforcement mechanisms. Doing so will require time and relentless effort, but strengthening the efficacy of international law so that it has greater meaning in the lives of the world's most dispossessed is possible. Indeed, it is a moral imperative. As the 5th century B.C. Greek historian and general Thucydides reminds us, there will be justice in Athens only when those who are not injured are as outraged as those who are.

PHOTOS

THE WEAPONS

U.S. B52 plane dropping bombs on Vietnam.

Project RENEW diorama depicting types of ordnance deployed during the Vietnam War.

Cluster bomb pod containing lethal bomblets like those deployed by the U.S. military. Bomblets continue to detonate upon human contact in family rice fields, gardens, and foot paths.

Samples of detonated cluster munitions dropped by the millions in Vietnam.

Cluster bomb bomblets remain deeply camouflaged in the soil throughout Vietnam, often detonated accidentally by farmers and their children.

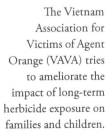

The Vietnam Association for Victims of Agent Orange (VAVA) tries to ameliorate the impact of long-term herbicide exposure on families and children.

Agent Orange spraying missions covered hundreds of thousands of acres across the country.

Entire forests were often defoliated by Agent Orange.

Agent Orange often leaked from its storage barrels at U.S. air bases across Vietnam.

A map of Vietnam with dark shading depicting the areas carpet-sprayed with Agent Orange during the War.

IMPACT OF WAR

Army veteran, Bui Trong Hong, of Project RENEW defusing a live bomb in Dakrong District, Quang Tri.

Removing UXO requires specially-trained teams to detect and physically remove unexploded ordnance.

The author's mother standing beside a bomb crater. Such craters are common throughout farmland and often are used as watering holes; a daily reminder of the perils of war.

A young boy and Project RENEW staff observe the spot where ordnance was removed from the grounds of a family home.

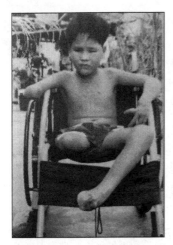

This young boy lost limbs after stepping on and detonating a buried mine.

Birth deformity in Vietnamese child believed to be due to Agent Orange exposure.

Prostheses for adults and children whose limbs have been blown off by left-behind cluster bombs and other ordnance.

UXO EDUCATION

Project RENEW staff teaches school children about the dangers of remaining ordnance.

A student identifies a cluster bomblet in a mine risk education program.

A child's drawing warns of remaining ordnance in her village.

VIETNAM: THE PEOPLE AND THE LAND

Fishermen ply their trade in waters once heavily polluted by U.S. herbicides.

Vegetable vendor at local market in Hoi An.

Farmers use water buffalo to plow fields still laden with unexploded bombs.

School children displaying a sense of normalcy where many others remain affected by the aftermath of the War.

Children in bamboo hut play normally but must be on alert for land mines and cluster bombs buried around their village.

Verdant rice fields produce crops twice per year, but on occasion yield explosive devices.

Four International Conventions Covered in Chapter 4

The following convention articles were selected for inclusion by the author for bearing greatest relevance to post-war cleanup and reparations responsibilities.

1. CONVENTION ON THE PROHIBITION OF MILITARY OR ANY OTHER HOSTILE USE OF ENVIRONMENTAL MODIFICATION TECHNIQUES (ENMOD) (1977)

Preamble:

Guided by the interest of consolidating peace, and wishing to contribute to the cause of halting the arms race, and of bringing about general and complete disarmament under strict and effective international control, and of saving mankind from the danger of using new means of warfare . . .

Determined to continue negotiations with a view to achieving effective progress toward further measures in the field of disarmament . . .

Recognizing, however, that military or any other hostile use of such techniques could have effects extremely harmful to human welfare . . .

Desiring to prohibit effectively military or any other hostile use of environmental modification techniques in order to eliminate the dangers to mankind from such use, and affirming their willingness to work towards the achievement of this objective . . .

Article 1 (1)—Each State Party to this Convention undertakes not to engage in military or any other hostile use of environmental modification techniques having widespread, long-lasting or severe effects as the means of destruction, damage or injury to any other State Party.

Article 2—As used in article I, the term environmental modification techniques refers to any technique for changing—through the deliberate manipulation of natural processes—the dynamics, composition or structure of the Earth, including its biota, lithosphere, hydrosphere and atmosphere, or of outer space.

Article 5 (5)—Each State Party to this Convention undertakes to provide or support assistance, in accordance with the provisions of the Charter of the United Nations, to any State Party which so requests, if the Security Council decides that such party has been harmed or is likely to be harmed as a result of violation of the Convention.

Understandings regarding the Convention—It is the understanding of the Committee that, for the purposes of this Convention, the terms "widespread", "long-lasting" and "severe" shall be interpreted as follows:

a) "widespread": encompassing an area on the scale of several hundred square kilometers

b) "long-lasting": lasting for a period of months, or approximately a season

c) "severe": involving serious or significant disruption or harm to human life, natural and economic resources or other assets.

2. CONVENTION ON THE PROHIBITION OF THE DEVELOPMENT, PRODUCTION, STOCKPILING AND USE OF CHEMICAL WEAPONS AND ON THEIR DESTRUCTION (CWC) (1997)

Article 1 (1) (c)—Each State Party to this Convention undertakes never under any circumstances to engage in any military preparations to use chemical weapons.

Article 1 (2)—Each State Party undertakes to destroy chemical weapons it owns or possesses, or that are located in any place under its jurisdiction or control, in accordance with the provisions of this Convention.

Article 1 (3)—Each State Party undertakes to destroy all chemical weapons it abandoned on the territory of another State Party, in accordance with the provisions of this Convention.

Article 1 (4)—Each State Party undertakes to destroy any chemical weapons production facilities it owns or possesses, or that are located in any place under its jurisdiction or control, in accordance with the provisions of this Convention.

Article 2 (1) (a)—"Chemical weapons" means toxic chemicals and their precursors, except where intended for purposes not prohibited under this Convention, as long as the types and quantities are consistent with such purposes . . .

Article 2 (2)—"Toxic Chemical" means any chemical which through its chemical action on life processes can cause death, temporary incapacitation or permanent harm to humans or animals. This includes all such chemicals, regardless of their origin or of their method of production, and regardless of whether they are produced in facilities, in munitions or elsewhere.

Article 2 (6)—"Abandoned Chemical Weapons" means chemical weapons, including old chemical weapons, abandoned by a State after 1 January 1925 on the territory of another State without the consent of the latter.

Article 2 (8) (a)—"Chemical Weapons Production Facility" means any equipment, as well as any building housing such equipment, that was designed, constructed or used at any time since 1 January 1946 . . .

Article 3 (1) (b)—With respect to old chemical weapons and abandoned chemical weapons:

(iii) Declare whether it has abandoned chemical weapons on the territory of other States and provide all available information in accordance with Part IV (B), paragraph 10, of the Verification Annex.

Article 3 (1) (c) (v)—With respect to chemical weapons production facilities: Provide its general plan for destruction of any chemical weapons production facility it owns or possesses, or that is located in any place under its jurisdiction or control, in accordance with Part V, paragraph 6, of the Verification Annex . . .

Article 3 (1) (c) (vi)—With respect to chemical weapons production facilities: Specify actions to be taken for closure of any chemical weapons production facility it owns or possesses, or that is located in any place under its jurisdiction or control, in accordance with Part V, paragraph 1 (i), of the Verification Annex . . .

Article 4 (6)—Each State Party shall destroy all chemical weapons specified in paragraph 1 pursuant to the Verification Annex and in accordance with the agreed rate and sequence of destruction (hereinafter referred to as "order of destruction"). Such destruction shall begin not later than two years after this Convention enters into force for it and shall finish not later than 10 years after entry into force of this Convention. A State Party is not precluded from destroying such chemical weapons at a faster rate.

Article 4 (7)—Each State Party shall:

(a) Submit detailed plans for the destruction of chemical weapons specified in paragraph 1 not later than 60 days before each annual destruction period begins, in accordance with Part IV (A), paragraph 29, of the Verification Annex; the detailed plans shall encompass all stocks to be destroyed during the next annual destruction period

(b) Submit declarations annually regarding the implementation of its plans for destruction of chemical weapons specified in paragraph 1, not later than 60 days after the end of each annual destruction period

(c) Certify, not later than 30 days after the destruction process has been completed, that all chemical weapons specified in paragraph 1 have been destroyed

Article 4 (11)—Any State Party which has on its territory chemical weapons that are owned or possessed by another State, or that are located in any place under the jurisdiction or control of another State, shall make the fullest efforts to ensure that these chemical weapons are removed from its territory not later than one year after this Convention enters into force for it. If they are not removed within one year, the State Party may request the Organization and other States Parties to provide assistance in the destruction of these chemical weapons.

Article 4 (12)—Each State Party undertakes to cooperate with other States Parties that request information or assistance on a bilateral basis or through the Technical Secretariat regarding methods and technologies for the safe and efficient destruction of chemical weapons.

Article 4 (16)—Each State Party shall meet the costs of destruction of chemical weapons it is obliged to destroy. It shall also meet the costs of verification of storage and destruction of these chemical weapons unless the Executive Council decides otherwise. If the Executive Council decides to limit verification measures of the Organization pursuant to paragraph 13, the costs of complementary verification and monitoring by the Organization shall be paid in accordance with the United Nations scale of assessment, as specified in Article VIII, paragraph 7.

Article 10 (8) (a)—Each State Party has the right to request and, subject to the procedures set forth in paragraphs 9, 10 and 11, to receive assistance and protection against the use or threat of use of chemical weapons if it considers that chemical weapons have been used against it . . .

3. CONVENTION ON CERTAIN CONVENTIONAL WEAPONS: PROTOCOL V ON EXPLOSIVE REMNANTS OF WAR (2006)

[It is noted that] the High Contracting Parties, recognizing the serious post-conflict humanitarian problems caused by explosive remnants of war [and] conscious of the need to conclude a Protocol on post-conflict remedial measures of a generic nature in order to minimize the risks and effects of explosive remnants of war . . . have agreed as follows . . ."

Article 1 (2)—This Protocol shall apply to explosive remnants of war on the land territory including internal waters of High Contracting Parties.

Article 2 (1)—Explosive ordnance means conventional munitions containing explosives, with the exception of mines, booby traps and other devices as defined in Protocol II of this Convention as amended on 3 May 1996.

Article 2 (2)—Unexploded ordnance means explosive ordnance that has been primed, fused, armed, or otherwise prepared for use and used in an armed conflict. It may have been fired, dropped, launched or projected and should have exploded but failed to do so.

Article 2 (5)—Existing explosive remnants of war means unexploded ordnance and abandoned explosive ordnance that existed prior to the entry into force of this Protocol for the [High Contracting Party on whose territory it exists].

Article 3 (1)—Each High Contracting Party and party to an armed conflict shall bear the responsibilities set out in this Article with respect to all explosive remnants of war in territory under its control. In cases where a user of explosive ordnance which has become explosive remnants of war, does not exercise control of the territory, the user shall, after the cessation of active hostilities, provide . . . inter alia technical, financial, material or human resources assistance . . . to facilitate the marking and clearance, removal or destruction of such explosive remnants of war. [Article 8(1) also obliges States Parties to "provide assistance for the marking and clearance, removal or destruction of explosive remnants of war."]

Article 3 (4)—In conducting the above activities High Contracting Parties and parties to an armed conflict shall take into account international standards, including the International Mine Action Standards. [Article 7(2) also obliges States Parties to "take into account the humanitarian objectives of this Protocol, as well as international standards . . ."].

Article 4 (1)—High Contracting Parties and parties to an armed conflict shall to the maximum extent possible and as far as practicable record and retain information on the use of explosive ordnance or abandonment of explosive ordnance, to facilitate the rapid marking and clearance, removal or destruction of explosive remnants of war, risk education and the provision of relevant information to the party in control of the territory and to civilian populations in that territory.

Article 4 (2)—High Contracting Parties and parties to an armed conflict which have used or abandoned explosive ordnance which may have become explosive remnants of war shall, without delay after the cessation of active hostilities and as far as practicable, subject to these parties' legitimate security interests, make available such information to the party or parties in control of the affected area, bilaterally or through a mutually agreed third party including inter alia the United Nations or, upon request, to other relevant organizations which the party providing the information is satisfied are or will be undertaking risk education and the marking and clearance, removal or destruction of explosive remnants of war in the affected area.

Article 7 (1)—Each High Contracting Party has the right to seek and receive assistance, where appropriate, from other High Contracting Parties, from states non-party and relevant international organizations and institutions in dealing with the problems posed by existing explosive remnants of war.

4. CONVENTION ON CLUSTER MUNITIONS (2010)

Article 2 (2)—Cluster munition means a conventional munition that is designed to disperse or release explosive sub-munitions each weighing less than 20 kilograms, and includes those explosive sub-munitions.

Article 4 (2) (d)—[Each State Party shall] . . . clear and destroy all cluster munition remnants located in areas under its jurisdiction or control.

Article 4 (4) (a)—This paragraph shall apply in cases in which cluster munitions have been used or abandoned by one State Party prior to entry into force of this Convention for that State Party and have become cluster munition remnants that are now located in areas under the jurisdiction or control of another State Party at the time of entry into force of this Convention for the latter. In such cases, upon entry into force of this Convention for both States Parties, the former State Party is strongly encouraged to provide, inter alia, technical, financial, material or human resources assistance to the latter State

Party . . . to facilitate the marking, clearance and destruction of such cluster munition remnants.

Article 4 (4) (b)—Such assistance shall include, where available, information on types and quantities of the cluster munitions used, precise locations of cluster munition strikes, and ones in which cluster munitions are known to be located.

Article 6 (3)— . . . The States Parties shall not impose undue restrictions on the provision and receipt of clearance and other such equipment and related technological information for humanitarian purposes.

Article 6 (6)—Where, after entry into force of this Convention, cluster munitions have become cluster munition remnants located in areas under the jurisdiction or control of a State Party, each State Party in a position to do so shall urgently provide emergency assistance to the affected State Party.

Article 21 (1)—Each State Party shall encourage States not party to this Convention to ratify, accept, approve or accede to this Convention, with the goal of attracting the adherence of all States to this Convention.

Major International Instruments Governing Armed Conflict and Post-War Obligations

This compilation of treaties, conventions, and world institutions was selected for their relevance to armed conflict, including conduct during war, protections for civilian populations, and obligations of States Parties for cleanup and reparation. Given the breadth of international law, this list is exemplary, not exhaustive.

The International Committee of the Red Cross (1863)—The world's largest humanitarian organization and the driving force behind the development of international humanitarian law. It oversees and ensures humanitarian protection and assistance for victims of armed conflict and other violence.

The Hague Conventions of 1899 and 1907—Multilateral treaties that were among the first formal statements of the laws of war, war crimes, and disarmament. The Conventions included a voluntary international court for compulsory arbitration to settle international disputes and established conditions for the belligerency of war as well as for the rights and obligations of persons in war.

Peace Treaty of Versailles (1919)—The treaty that effectively ended the First World War. It required "Germany [to] accept the responsibility of Germany and her allies for causing all the loss and damage" during the War and forced the nation to disarm, make substantial territorial concessions, and pay reparations.

The League of Nations (1920)—The first international organization established to maintain world peace through collective security and disarmament, settling international disputes through negotiation and arbitration. Other issues in this and related treaties included labor conditions, just treatment of native inhabitants, human and drug trafficking, the arms trade, global health, prisoners of war, and protection of minorities in Europe.

The Geneva Protocol of 1925 (Protocol for the Prohibition of the Use in War of Asphyxiating, Poisonous or Other Gases, and of Bacteriological Methods of Warfare)—A treaty drawing upon the language of The Peace Treaty of Versailles to prohibit the use of chemical and biological weapons in international armed conflicts.

Charter of the United Nations (1945)—The founding treaty of the United Nations, of which the Statute of the International Court of Justice is an integral part. The Charter was created in the wake of war to reaffirm the global commitment to human rights. Its Preamble states that force shall not be used unless it's in the common interest.

International Court of Justice (1945)—The ICJ was established in 1945 by the UN Charter. It is the primary judicial branch of the United Nations; all state members of the United Nations are automatically parties to the Court's statute. In accordance with international law, it decides legal disputes submitted to it by States.

Geneva Conventions of 1949—The Conventions establish the conduct of states in armed conflict and protections for civilians.

European Court of Justice (1959)—The highest court in the European Union in matters of European Union law. It is tasked with interpreting EU law and ensuring its equal application across all EU member states.

ENMOD Convention (1977)—As part of disarmament efforts, this convention prohibits States Parties from engaging in military or any other hostile use of environmental modification techniques having widespread, long-lasting or severe effects as the means of destruction, damage, or injury to any other State Party.

Inter-American Court of Human Rights (1979)—The Court enforces and interprets the provisions of the American Convention on Human Rights. Its two main functions are adjudicatory and advisory.

Convention on Conventional Weapons (1983)—Restricts or bans the use of specific types of weapons that cause unnecessary or unjustifiable suffering to combatants, or that affect civilians indiscriminately.

International Criminal Tribunal for the former Yugoslavia (ICTY, 1993)—An ad hoc court in The Hague that prosecuted war crimes committed during the Balkan Wars in the 1990s.

Chemical Weapons Convention (1997)—Prohibits the development, production, acquisition, stockpiling, retention, transfer or use of chemical weapons by States Parties.

International Criminal Court (1998)—The ICC is a treaty court established to prosecute individuals responsible for crimes of genocide, crimes against humanity, and war crimes.

African Court of Human and Peoples' Rights (2004)—The Court ensures respect for and compliance with the African Charter on Human and Peoples' Rights, as well as other international human rights instruments, through judicial decisions.

Protocol V of the Convention on Certain Conventional Weapons (2006)—The first multilateral instrument to establish a clear rule that explosive munitions must be cleared once hostilities have ceased.

Convention on Cluster Munitions (2010)—Prohibits the use, production, transfer, and stockpiling of cluster munitions, addresses harm to civilians caused by such munitions, and assigns responsibility to respective States Parties for the cleanup of cluster munitions.

Obligation of Appropriated Funds for Agent Orange/Dioxin Related Activities in Vietnam by Fiscal Year and Type of Activity

The following two-page table was provided by USAID as of May 29, 2014.

Program Component/Activity	Implementing Partner	FY2007	FY2008	FY2009	FY2010	FY2011	FY2012	FY2013	TOTAL
HEALTH/DISABILITY									
Empowering People with Disabilities in Danang	Save the Children (SC)	400,000	-	799,980	-	-	-	-	1,199,980
Rehabilitation Services and Socioeconomic Support to People with Disabilities in Danang	Vietnam Assistance for the Handicapped (VNAH)	382,344	-	906,064	-	-	-	-	1,288,408
Support of People with Disabilities in Danang	East Meets West Foundation (EMW)	200,000	-	300,000	-	-	-	-	500,000
Disability Support Program	Development Alternatives Inc. (DAI)	-	-	-	-	5,192,582	2,477,342	-	7,669,924
Disability/Health Assessment	Chemonics	-	-	-	103,000	-	-	-	103,000
Disability/Health Support Inter-agency Agreement (IAA)	Center for Disease Control (CDC)	-	-	-	-	53,169	-	-	53,169
Program Support	USAID	17,656	96,102	118,009	100,000	70,907	200,000	75,000	677,674
Subtotal Health/Disability		1,000,000	96,102	2,124,053	203,000	5,316,658	2,677,342	75,000	11,492,155
ENVIRONMENTAL REMEDIATION									
Assessments and Engineering Designs and Plans for Dioxin Remediation at Danang Airport	CDM International, Inc.	-	1,450,000	681,076	2,411,200	-	-	-	4,542,276
Excavation and Construction Services for Dioxin Remediation at Danang Airport	Tetra Tech, Inc.	-	-	-	5,429,408	11,566,804	-	-	16,996,212

Program Component/Activity	Implementing Partner	FY2007	FY2008	FY2009	FY2010	FY2011	FY2012	FY2013	TOTAL
In-pile Thermal Desorption (IPTD) Design for Dioxin Remediation at Danang Airport	TerraTherm, Inc.	-	-	-	-	1,336,486	-	-	1,336,486
In-pile Thermal Desorption Implementation for Dioxin Remediation at Danang Airport	Tetra Therm, Inc.	-	-	-	-	-	16,492,658	11,209,712	27,702,370
Construction Management Oversight of Remediation at Danang Airport	CDM International Inc.	-	-	-	6,000,000	2,336,444	-	-	8,336,444
Bien Hoa Environment Assessment	CDM International, Inc.	-	-	-	-	-	5,200	500,000	505,200
Program Support	USAID	-	453,898	194,871	300,000	463,000	824,800	489,430	2,725,999
Subtotal Environmental Remediation		-	1,903,898	875,947	14,140,608	15,702,734	17,322,658	12,199,142	62,144,987
Total Health/Disability and Environmental Remediation Program		1,000,000	2,000,000	3,000,000	14,343,608	21,019,392	20,000,000	12,274,142	73,637,142

Source: USAID, as of May 29, 2014.

Notes: USAID was unable to provide CRS with updated obligation data for FY2013 and FY2014 in time for inclusion in this report.

Glossary

Abandoned chemical weapons: Chemical weapons, abandoned by a state after 1 January 1925, on the territory of another state without the consent of the latter.

Accede/Accession: An act by which a state signifies its agreement to be legally bound by the terms of a particular treaty. Accession has the same legal effect as ratification but is not preceded by an act of signature.

Adoption: The formal act by which the form and content of a proposed treaty text are established by the UN.

Binding: A term used to indicate that once a state ratifies a convention it is legally bound to it under international law.

Bomblets: Small bombs stored in a mother lode.

Chemical weapons: Toxic chemicals and their precursors, such as mustard gas.

Cluster munition/cluster bomb: A conventional munition that is designed to disperse or release explosive sub-munitions, each weighing less than 20 kilograms and containing pieces of shrapnel.

Compliance gap: A reference to states falling short of implementing treaty obligations to which they are legally bound.

Convention: A formal agreement between states. The generic term 'convention' is synonymous with the generic term 'treaty.' Conventions are typically open for participation by the international community as a whole, or by a large number of states. Conventions are stronger than Declarations because they are legally binding for governments that have ratified them.

Customary international law: Refers to international obligations arising from established state practices, as opposed to obligations arising from formal written international treaties. According to Article 38(1)(b) of the Statute of the International Court of Justice, customary international law is one of the sources of international law. Customary international law can be established by demonstrating (1) a general and consistent practice of states, and (2) *opinio juris* (a sense of legal obligation).

Declaration: A document that states agreed-upon global standards but is not legally binding.

Entry into force: The process by which legal instruments (legislation, regulations, treaties and others) come into force for States Parties. A treaty typically enters into force at a specified time following its ratification or accession by a fixed number of states.

Environmental modification technique: Any technique for changing or influencing the dynamics, composition or structure of the Earth, including its biota, lithosphere, hydrosphere and atmosphere, or of outer space, through the deliberate manipulation of natural processes.

Ex post facto: Application of laws that provide for the infliction of sanctions upon a person or state for some prior act that, at the time it was committed, was not illegal. In Latin, the term means "from a thing done after the fact."

Explosive Remnants of War (ERW): Unexploded ordnance and abandoned explosive ordnance left by a state on the territory of another state following the cessation of formal hostilities.

Explosive ordnance: Conventional munitions containing explosives, with the exception of mines, booby traps, and other devices.

Geneva Conventions of 1949: An initial step, under international law, toward mitigating the barbarity of war and establishing stronger civilian protections during armed conflict. See Appendix B for more detail.

Hague Conventions of 1899 and 1907: Conventions that govern the use of weapons against civilian populations, prohibit the employment of arms that can cause superfluous injury, and prohibit attacks on undefended villages. See Appendix B for more detail.

Human rights treaty bodies: UN-based committees of independent experts who monitor and issue reports on States Parties' implementation of the major human rights treaties they have ratified.

International NGOs: Private, non-governmental organizations whose purpose is to facilitate, prod, and pressure states into greater compliance with their human rights obligations.

Jus cogens: Considered by some as "super" customary international law—international law so fundamental to the inter-relationship of states that a state cannot, through its treaty practice or otherwise, deviate from the law. Because of the overarching importance of *jus cogens* norms, it is generally accepted among courts and scholars that there are only a limited number of them, including genocide, slavery, and torture.

Opinio juris: In customary international law, *opinio juris* is one of two elements (along with state practice) necessary to establish a legally binding standard. *Opinio juris* denotes a widespread sense of obligation irrespective of independent treaty law.

Optional Protocol: Optional Protocols to human rights treaties are separate from the treaties themselves and include specific additional obligations open to signature, accession, or ratification by countries regardless of their ratification status to the main treaty. For example, the U.S. ratified the two Optional Protocols of the Convention on the Rights of the Child but it has not ratified the treaty.

Protocol: The term to describe agreements of a less formal nature than treaties or conventions. Generally, a protocol amends, supplements, or clarifies a multilateral treaty. While it is linked to the parent agreement, a protocol can focus on a specific aspect of that agreement in greater detail. For example, the Convention on the Rights of the Child includes a protocol on the involvement of children in armed conflict.

Ratification: An act by which a state becomes legally bound by the terms of a particular treaty. To ratify a treaty, a state's administrative apparatus first signs it and then fulfils its own national legislative approval requirements. In the U.S., for example, this means approval by the Senate.

Reparations: An established practice that acknowledges the legal obligation of a state or entity to repair the consequence of rights violations or abuses, whether due to direct involvement or because of failure to prevent them. International law now recognizes several forms of reparations including restitution, compensation and rehabilitation, and the guarantee of non-repetition.

Reservation: A method for states to exempt themselves from committing to specified treaty provisions (articles) they claim are incompatible with internal laws and/or customs.

Retroactivity: The application of treaty law to state obligations or actions prior to entry into force of a particular treaty.

Signing/Signatory to a treaty: An administrative pledge or intention by a government to later comply with the treaty. The act of signing a treaty is not legally binding, as it must then be ratified.

Scofflaw: One who ignores or flouts the law, especially laws difficult to enforce.

Special UN rapporteurs: Individuals who, in addition to monitoring the implementation of particular subject matter covered by treaty provisions, provide recommendations and technical knowledge to help move states toward greater compliance.

States Parties: Countries that have ratified a particular treaty, and are therefore legally bound by its provisions.

Toxic chemical: Any chemical that, through its chemical action on life processes, can cause death, temporary incapacitation, or permanent harm to humans, animals, plants, or other living things.

Treaty: A formally concluded and ratified agreement between states. The term is used generically to refer to instruments binding under international law, concluded between international entities (states or organizations). Under the Vienna Conventions on the Law of Treaties, a treaty must be (1) a binding instrument, which means that the contracting parties intend to create legal rights and duties; (2) concluded by states or international organizations with treaty-making power; (3) governed by international law; and (4) set down in writing.

Treaty of Versailles (1919): This treaty was concluded after World War I by instituting an accord between Germany and the Allied Powers that established guidelines for continued peace. See Appendix B for more detail.

Unexploded Ordnance (UXO): Explosive ordnance that have been primed, fused, armed, or otherwise prepared for use and employed in an armed conflict, but failed to detonate on impact. They may have been fired, dropped, launched, or projected to explode but failed to do so.

Universal Declaration of Human Rights (UDHR): A milestone document in the history of human rights. Drafted by representatives with different legal and cultural backgrounds from all regions of the world, the Declaration is a common standard of achievements for all peoples and all nations. It sets out, for the first time, fundamental human rights to be universally protected and has been translated into over 500 languages. The UDHR was established in 1948 and is generally considered the foundation for international human rights law.

Sources

Many of the preceding definitions were adapted from the following sources between 2015 and 2017:

Print

- *The Concise Oxford Dictionary of Current English* (8th edition), Clarendon Press, Oxford, 1990

Online

- http://www.duhaime.org/LegalDictionary/P/Protocol.aspx
- http://www.judicialmonitor.org/archive_1206/generalprinciples.html
- https://www.law.cornell.edu/wex/customary_international_law
- https://www.law.cornell.edu/wex/ex_post_facto
- https://www.law.cornell.edu/wex/opinio_juris_international_law
- http://legal-dictionary.thefreedictionary.com/Ex+Post+Facto+Laws
- https://treaties.un.org/pages/overview.aspx?path=overview/glossary/page1_en.xml
- http://www.un.org/womenwatch/daw/cedaw/protocol/whatis.htm
- United Nations Treaty Collection, Treaty Reference Guide, 1999, available at http://untreaty.un.org/English/guide.asp

Endnotes

Chapter 1

1. Judy Gumbo, "Viet Nam Time Travel," Chapter 2; Ngo Xuan Hien and Nguyen Thanh Phu (Project RENEW staff) in discussion with the author, July 2016.

2. James P. Harrison, "History's Heaviest Bombing." In *The Vietnam War: Vietnamese and American Perspectives*, edited by Jayne S. Werner and Luu Doan Huynh (New York: Routledge, 1994), p. 133; Michael Clodfelter. *Vietnam in Military Statistics: A History of the Indochina Wars 1772–1991* (Jefferson: McFarland and Company, Inc., 1995).

3. "America Launches Operation Rolling Thunder," accessed June 12, 2016. http://www.history.com/topics/vietnam-war/operation-rolling-thunder.

4. Kolko. *Anatomy of a War*, p. 457.

5. "Minh Surrenders: Viet Cong in Saigon." *New York Times*. April 30, 1975, p.1.

6. James P. Harrison, "History's Heaviest Bombing," p. 130–139.

7. Ben Kiernan and Taylor Owen, "Making More Enemies Than We Kill? Calculating U.S. Bomb Tonnages Dropped on Laos and Cambodia, and Weighing Their Implications," *Japan Focus: The Asia-Pacific Journal* 13, no. 17 (2015), p. 1–3.

8. Chuck Searcy (founder of Project RENEW) in discussion with the author, July 2016 (citing Department of Defense data); "U.S. Veteran Leads Clean-up of Vietnam War's Lethal Remnants," *PBS Newshour* (November 20, 2014), accessed September 17, 2016. http://www.pbs.org/newshour/bb/u-s-veteran-leads-clean-vietnam-wars-lethal-remnants; "Cluster Bomb Fact Sheet," Legacies of War, accessed September 3, 2016, http://legaciesofwar.org/resources/cluster-bomb-fact-sheet, p. 1.

9. "Hard to Clear Post-War Bombs and Mines," *Vietnam Government Portal: Online Newspaper of the Government*, May 14, 2012, accessed June 21, 2016, http://news.chinhphu.vn/Home/Hard-to-clear-postwar-bombs-and-mines/20125/14389.vgp, p. 1.

10. International Committee of the Red Cross, "Explosive Remnants of War," *International Committee of the Red Cross Resource Center*, 2014.

11. Myra MacPherson, "Voices of Veterans: The Endless Tragedy of Vietnam." In *The People Make the Peace: Lessons from the Vietnam Antiwar Movement,* edited by Karín Aguilar-San Juan and Frank Joyce (Charlottesville: Just World Books, 2015).

12. Arnold Schecter et al., "Recent Dioxin Contamination from Agent Orange in Residents of a Southern Vietnam City," *Journal of Occupational and Environmental Medicine* 43, no. 1 (2001), p. 1; Michael F Martin, "U.S. Agent Orange/Dioxin Assistance to Vietnam," *Congressional Research Service*, 2015, accessed September 17, 2016, https://fas.org/sgp/crs/row/R44268.pdf, p. 1.

13. Charles Bailey, "Agent Orange: What Efforts Are Being Made to Address the Continuing Impact of Dioxin in Vietnam?" Written

testimony prepared for The House Committee on Foreign Affairs Subcommittee on Asia, the Pacific and the Global Environment, Washington, DC, June 2009, p. 7; Annika Johansson and Le Thi Nham Tuyet, "Impact of Chemical Warfare with Agent Orange on Women's Reproductive Lives in Vietnam: A Pilot Study," *Reproductive Health Matters* 9 no. 18 (2001), p. 156.

14. This figure is the official U.S. Defense Department estimate, as quoted in Charles Hirschman et al., "Vietnamese Casualties During the American War: A New Estimate," *Population and Development Review* 21 no. 4 (1995), p. 790

15. The Encyclopedia of the Vietnam War: A Political, Social, and Military History. 2nd edition. Ed. Spencer C. Tucker, p. 175.

16. The Encyclopedia of the Vietnam War: A Political, Social, and Military History. 2nd edition. Ed. Spencer C. Tucker, p. 175; Clarke, Jeffrey J. (1988), *United States Army in Vietnam: Advice and Support: The Final Years, 1965–1973*, Washington, D.C: Center of Military History, United States Army, p. 275; R.J. Rummel, "Vietnam Democide, Estimates, Sources and Calculations." University of Hawaii, accessed August 1, 2016. http://www.hawaii.edu/powerkills/SOD.TAB6.1A.GIF, line 129.

17. R.J. Rummel, "Vietnam Democide, Estimates, Sources and Calculations." University of Hawaii, accessed August 1, 2016. http://www.hawaii.edu/powerkills/SOD.TAB6.1A.GIF, line 129.

18. *The Encyclopedia of the Vietnam War: A Political, Social, and Military History.* 5th edition. Edited by Dr. Spencer Tucker, and Dr. Paul G. Pierpaoli Jr (Santa Barbara: ABC-CLIO, 2011), p. 176.

19. Lewy, *America in Vietnam*, p. 453.

20. *The Encyclopedia of the Vietnam War: A Political, Social, and Military History.* 5th edition, p. 176.

21. National Archives, *Military Records: Statistical Information About Fatal Casualties of the Vietnam War*, accessed June 11, 2016,

http://www.archives.gov/research/military/vietnam-war/casualty-statistics.html. See "Casualty Category."

Chapter 2

1. Ross Wilson, *The Language of the Past* (New York: Bloomsbury Publishing Place, 2016), p. 61.

2. "Explosive Remnants of War," *International Committee of the Red Cross Resource Center*, p. 1.

3. Ibid, p.1.

4. Wells-Dang, "A Regional Approach", p. 1.

5. "Cluster Bombs", *Handicap International United Kingdom*, accessed July 10, 2016, http://www.handicap-international.us/cluster_bombs, p. 1.

6. George Black, "The Vietnam War is Still Killing People," *The New Yorker*, May 20, 2016, p. 3.

7. "Cluster Bombs", *Handicap International, p. 1*; George Black, "The Vietnam War is Still Killing People", p. 3.

8. "Cluster Bombs," *Handicap International, p. 2*.

9. "Cluster Bombs," *Handicap International, p. 2*.

10. Chuck Searcy, "US Veteran Leads Clean-Up of Vietnam War's Lethal Remnants," *PBS Newshour* (November 20, 2014), accessed October 16, 2016, http://www.pbs.org/newshour/bb/u-s-veteran-leads-clean-vietnam-wars-lethal-remnants.

11. Olson, "A New Approach," p. 3.

12. Doug Hostetter, "A Pacifist in the War Zone." In *The People Make the Peace: Lessons from the Vietnam Antiwar Movement,* edited by Karín Aguilar-San Juan and Frank Joyce (Charlottesville: Just World Books, 2015), p. 107–120; Chuck Searcy (founder of Project RENEW) in discussion with the author, June 28, 2016; Olson, "A New Approach," p. 2.

13. Jonathon Guthrie and Portia Stratton, "The Quang Tri Integrated Survey and Clearance Project," *The Journal of ERW and Mine Action*, 19.1, April 2015, p. 16.

14. Interview with Ngo Xuan Hien and Nguyen Thanh Phu (Project RENEW staff) in discussion with the author, June 27, 2016.

15. Interview with Ngo Xuan Hien and Nguyen Thanh Phu, 2016; Wyatt Olson, "A New Approach to Ridding Vietnam of Unexploded Ordnance," *Stars and Stripes,* accessed June 27, 2016. https://www. stripes.com/news/pacific/a-new-approach-to-ridding-vietnam-of-unexploded-ordnance-1.176497#.WOPixqK1tPZ, p. 2.

16. Landmine and Cluster Munition Monitor. "Vietnam: Casualties and Victim Assistance." 2015. Accessed October 16, 2016, http://www.the-monitor.org/en-gb/reports/2017/vietnam/casualties-and-victim-assistance.aspx.

17. Olson, "A New Approach."

18. Andrew Wells-Dang, "A Regional Approach: Mine and UXO Risk Reduction in Vietnam, Laos and Cambodia," *Journal of Mine Action* No. 9.2 (2013), accessed July 7, 2016, http://www.jmu.edu/cisr/journal/9.2/focus/wells-dang/wells-dang.shtml, p. 3.

19. Chloe Cunningham, "U.S. and Vietnam Sign Memorandum of Understanding," *The Journal of ERW and Mine Action,* 18.1, Spring 2014, p. 1.

20. "Deputy Defense Minister Nguyen Chi Vinh Talks About VN-US Defense Ties," *Vietnam Net Bridge*, March 3, 2015. Accessed May 3, 2016. http://english.vietnamnet.vn/fms/special-reports/126759/deputy-defense-minister-nguyen-chi-vinh-talks-about-vn-us-defense-ties.html, p. 4; Olson, "A New Approach."

21. "Explosive Remnants of War," *International Committee of the Red Cross Resource Center,* accessed August 16, 2016, https://shop.icrc.org/les-restes-explosifs-de-guerre.html?___store=default, p. 4.

22. Ibid, p. 4.

23. Ibid, p. 4.

24. Ibid, p. 6.

25. Ibid, p. 6.

26. Wells-Dang, "A Regional Approach", p. 3.

27. Wendy Waldeck and Sarah Sensamaust, "Vietnam," *Journal of Mine Action*, No. 9.2 (2006), accessed July 11, 2016, http://www.jmu.edu/cisr/journal/9.2/profiles/vietnam/vietnam.shtml, p. 1.

28. Interview with Ngo Xuan Hien and Nguyen Thanh Phu, 2016.

29. Interview with Ngo Xuan Hien and Nguyen Thanh Phu, 2016.

30. *Interactions with a Violent Past: Reading Post-Conflict Landscapes in Cambodia, Laos, and Vietnam, edited by* Vatthana Pholsena and Oliver Tappe (Singapore: National University of Singapore Press, 2013), p. 55.

31. Wells-Dang, "A Regional Approach," p. 2.

32. Interview with Ngo Xuan Hien and Nguyen Thanh Phu, 2016; Olson, "A New Approach," p. 3.

33. Quang Tri Province Legacy of War Coordination Center website, accessed June 14, 2016, http://lwcc-dbu-quangtri.vn/en-us/FACTS-AND-FIGURES/By-Province/Quang-Tri-Province, p. 1.

34. "Explosive Remnants of War Accidents and Casualties in Quang Tri from 2000–2016," Project RENEW website, accessed July 20, 2016, http://www.landmines.org.vn.

35. Interview with Searcy, 2016.

36. Interview with Searcy, 2016.

37. Interview with Searcy, 2016.

38. Interview with Ngo Xuan Hien and Nguyen Thanh Phu, 2016.

39. Interview with Searcy, 2016.

40. Interview with Searcy, 2016.

41. Olson, "A New Approach", p. 4.

42. Interview with Searcy, 2016.

43. Interview with Searcy, 2016.

44. Interview with Searcy, 2016.

45. Interview with Ngo Xuan Hien and Nguyen Thanh Phu, 2016.

46. Interview with Ngo Xuan Hien and Nguyen Thanh Phu, 2016.

47. Interview with Ngo Xuan Hien and Nguyen Thanh Phu, 2016.

Chapter 3

1. Schecter, "Recent Dioxin Contamination from Agent," p. 435–443; Jeanne Stellman, "The Extent and Patterns of Usage of Agent Orange and Other Herbicides in Vietnam," *Nature* 422 (2003), p. 681.

2. George Black, "The Lethal Legacy of the Vietnam War," *The Nation,* March 16, 2015, p. 22–23.

3. "Spillover," Agent Orange Record, accessed June 22, 2016, http://www.agentorangerecord.com/impact_on_vietnam/environment/hot_spots, p. 1.

4. Stellman, "The Extent and Patterns," p. 681; Black, "The Lethal Legacy," p. 23.

5. Stellman, "The Extent and Patterns," p. 682.

6. "The Invisible Enemy," *Agent Orange Record,* accessed July 1, 2016, http://www.agentorangerecord.com/agent_orange_history/in_vietnam, p.1.

7. Stellman (quoted in George Black, "The Lethal Legacy," p. 22.

8. Stellman, "The Extent and Patterns," p. 681; Hatfield Consultants, Ltd, "Preliminary Assessment of Environmental Impacts Related to Spraying of Agent Orange Herbicide During the Viet Nam War," 1998, accessed July 11, 2016, http://www.hatfieldgroup.

com/wp-content/uploads/AgentOrangeReports/CIDA614/default.
htm, p. 36–38; John Stapleton, *Agent Orange: The Cleanup Begins,*
(Sydney: A Sense of Place Publishing, Inc, 2013), p.6–7.

9. "Promoting Hope and Dignity: A Long-Term Humanitarian
Response to Agent Orange and Dioxin in Vietnam," *The Aspen
Institute,* accessed July 11, 2016, https://www.aspeninstitute.org/
programs/agent-orange-in-vietnam-program/promoting-hope-
dignity-long-term-humanitarian-response-agent-orange-dioxin-
vietnam, p. 2; Stapleton, *Agent Orange: The Cleanup Begins,* p. 7.

10. "What is Agent Orange?" *The Aspen Institute,* accessed July 7,
2016, https://www.aspeninstitute.org/programs/agent-orange-in-
vietnam-program/what-is-agent-orange, p.4; The War Remnants
Museum, Ho Chi Minh City, Vietnam, 2016.

11. "Agent Orange," *The American Public Health Association,* accessed
July 7, 2016, https://www.apha.org/policies-and-advocacy/public-
health-policy-statements/policy-database/2014/07/29/13/22/agent-
orange, p. 1; Program staff (Vietnamese Association for Victims of
Agent Orange) in discussion with the author, July 2016.

12. "Eating, Drinking, Touching, Breathing, Nursing, Conceiving,"
The Agent Orange Record, accessed June 10, 2016, http://www.
agentorangerecord.com/impact_on_vietnam/health, p. 4.

13. "Dioxins and Their Effects on Human Health," *World Health
Organization,* accessed July 8, 2016, http://www.who.int/
mediacentre/factsheets/fs225/en, Section: "Key Facts."

14. Doug Hostetter, "A Pacifist in the War Zone." In *The People Make
the Peace: Lessons from the Vietnam Antiwar Movement,* edited by
Karín Aguilar-San Juan and Frank Joyce (Charlottesville, Just
World Books: 2015); Johansson and Le, "Impact of Chemical
Warfare," p. 156.

15. Schecter, "Recent Dioxin Contamination," p. 435; "Dioxins and
Their Effects on Human Health," *World Health Organization,*

Section: "Background;" "Dioxins," *The National Institute of Environmental Health Science*, accessed July 14, 2016, https://www.niehs.nih.gov/health/topics/agents/dioxins, p. 1.

16. "All You Ever Wanted to Know About Dioxin or Perhaps You Really Do Not Want to Know," *Agent Orange Association of Canada*, accessed July 19, 2016, http://www.agentorangecanada.com/dioxin.php, p. 1.

17. "Health Effects," *The Aspen Institute*, accessed June 10, 2016, https://www.aspeninstitute.org/programs/agent-orange-in-vietnam-program/health-effects, p. 4; Charles Bailey and Susan Hammond, "Frequently Asked Questions About Agent Orange/Dioxin," *War Legacies Project and Ford Foundation*, accessed June 9, 2016, http://www.agentorangerecord.com/images/uploads/modules/AODFAQ.pdf, p. 4.

18. "What is Agent Orange?" *The Aspen Institute*, p. 4.

19. Tran Thi Tuyet-Hanh et al, "Environmental Health Risk Assessment of Dioxin Exposure Through Foods in a Dioxin Hot Spot—Bien Hoa City, Vietnam," *International Journal of Environmental Research and Public Health*, 7 no. 5 (2010), p. 2397.

20. Tran, "Environmental Health Risk Assessment, p. 2398.

21. "All You Ever Wanted to Know About Dioxin," *Agent Orange Association of Canada*, p. 2.

22. Tran, "Environmental Health Risk Assessment, p. 2397.

23. Stellman, "The Extent and Patterns," p. 685.

24. Laws, Edward A, *Aquatic Pollution: An Introductory Text 3rd edition* (Los Angeles: John Wiley & Sons, 2000), 354; The War Remnants Museum, Ho Chi Minh City, Vietnam, 2016.

25. Stellman, "The Extent and Patterns," p. 685.

26. Tran, "Environmental Health Risk Assessment," p. 2396.

27. Tran, "Environmental Health Risk Assessment," p. 2397.

28. "The Chemical Scythe," *Agent Orange Record*, accessed July 15, 2016, http://www.agentorangerecord.com/impact_on_vietnam/environment/defoliation, p. 1.

29. "The Chemical Scythe," *Agent Orange Record*, p. 2.

30. Schecter, "Recent Dioxin Contamination," p. 442.

31. Bailey and Hammond, "Frequently Asked Questions," p. 4.

32. Bailey and Hammond, "Frequently Asked Questions," p. 4.

33. Black, "The Lethal Legacy," p. 24–25.

34. Martha Hamilton, "First of Monsanto Workers' Agent Orange Trials Is Set," *The Washington Post,* accessed July 15, 2016, https://www.washingtonpost.com/archive/business/1984/06/10/first-of-monsanto-workers-agent-orange-trials-is-set/52f2d640-d050-4325-a939-2043a937830f/?utm_term=.b26b837418dc, p. 3.

35. "All You Ever Wanted to Know About Dioxin," *Agent Orange Association of Canada,* p. 4–5; Brant Hamel, "Dioxin Exposure Causes Transgenerational Health Effects," *National Institute of Environmental Health Sciences* 120, no. 11 (2012), p. 1.

36. "Health Effects," *The Aspen Institute*, p. 1.

37. Arnold, Schecter, "Statement to the House Subcommittee on Asia, the Pacific and the Global Environment on the impact of Agent Orange." Vietnam Agent Orange Relief and Responsibility Campaign, Washington, DC, May 2008, p. 1.

38. Hamel, "Dioxin Exposure," p. 1–2.

39. Hamel, "Dioxin Exposure," p. 2.

40. MacPherson, *The People Make the Peace*, p. 192.

41. Black, "The Lethal Legacy," p. 30.

42. Dang Duc Nhu et al, "A GIS Study of Dioxin Contamination in a Vietnamese Region Sprayed with Herbicide," *Environmental Health and Preventive Medicine* 14, no. 6 (2009), p. 356.

43. Schecter, "Recent Dioxin Contamination," p. 435.

44. Marjorie Cohn, "Agent Orange: Terrible Legacy of the Vietnam War," Thomas Jefferson School of Law, *The Huffington Post*, May 1, 2016, p. 2.

45. Hamel, "Dioxin Exposure," p. 1.

46. "Health Effects," *The Aspen Institute*, p. 3.

47. "Health Effects," *The Aspen Institute*, p. 2.

48. *Chau, Beyond the Lines*, directed by Courtney Marsh (2015; Los Angeles, CA: Seventh Art Releasing).

49. Black, "The Lethal Legacy," p. 14.

50. Stellman. "The Extent and Patterns," p. 681.

51. Black, "The Lethal Legacy," p. 25.

52. Stellman, "The Extent and Patterns," p. 686.

53. Stellman, "The Extent and Patterns," p. 685.

54. Stellman, "The Extent and Patterns," p. 682.

55. Declan Butler, "Flight Records Reveal Full Extent of Agent Orange Contamination in Vietnam," *Nature* 422, no. 6933 (2003), accessed June 11, 2016, http://www.nature.com/news/2003/030417/full/news030414-10.html, p. 2.

56. Butler, "Flight Records," p. 2.

57. Hatfield Consultants, "Preliminary Assessment," p. 31.

58. Hatfield Consultants, Ltd, "Identification of New Agent Orange/Dioxin Contamination Hot Spots in Southern Viet Nam: Final Report," 2006, p. 1–2.

59. Charles Bailey, "Agent Orange: What Efforts Are Being Made to Address the Continuing Impact of Dioxin in Vietnam?" Written testimony prepared for The House Committee on Foreign Affairs Subcommittee on Asia, the Pacific and the Global Environment, Washington, DC, June 2009, p. 18.

60. Michael F. Martin, "U.S. Agent Orange/Dioxin Assistance to Vietnam," *Congressional Research Service*, 2015, accessed August 5, 2016, https://fas.org/sgp/crs/row/R44268.pdf, p. 1.

61. Hatfield Consultants, "Preliminary Assessment," p. 12.

62. Schecter, "Recent Dioxin Contamination," p. 435.

63. Schecter, "Recent Dioxin Contamination," p. 435.

64. L.W. Dwernychuk et al, "The Agent Orange Dioxin Issue in Viet Nam: A Manageable Problem," The International Symposium on Halogenated Persistent Organic Pollutants, 2006, accessed July 16, 2016, http://www.vn-agentorange.org/edmaterials/oslo_fcc-2602-378231.pdf, p. 1.

65. Stellman, "The Extent and Patterns," p. 681.

66. "Hot Spots: Cleaning Up Dioxin-Contaminated Soils," *The Aspen Institute*, accessed July 10, 2016, https://assets.aspeninstitute.org/content/uploads/files/content/docs/agent-orange/4AOVIIFact Sheet-HotSpots-CleaningUpDioxin-ContaminatedSoils-Aug2011.pdf, p. 2.

67. Bailey, "Agent Orange," p. 20.

68. Bailey, "Agent Orange," p. 20–21.

69. Bailey, "Agent Orange," p. 21.

70. Martin, "U.S. Agent Orange/Dioxin Assistance," p. 1. (See also "Ford Foundation's Landmark Work on Agent Orange Transitions to Aspen Institute," *The Ford Foundation*, May 5, 2011, accessed June 22, 2016, http://www.fordfoundation.org/the-latest/news/ford-foundations-landmark-work-on-agent-orange-transitions-to-aspen-institute; Bailey, "Agent Orange.")

71. Bailey, "Agent Orange," p. 11.

72. Martin, "U.S. Agent Orange/Dioxin Assistance," p. 3.

73. Martin, "U.S. Agent Orange/Dioxin Assistance," p. 4.

74. "Clean Up Efforts," *The Aspen Institute*, August 2011, accessed July 10, 2016, https://www.aspeninstitute.org/programs/agent-orange-in-vietnam-program/cleaning-up-contaminated-soil, p. 4.

75. Senator Leahy's War Victim Fund (as quoted in Michael F Martin, "U.S. Agent Orange/Dioxin Assistance to Vietnam," *Congressional Research Service*, p. 12.)

76. Martin, "U.S. Agent Orange/Dioxin Assistance," p. 12.

77. *Chau, Beyond the Lines*, 2015.

78. Martin, "U.S. Agent Orange/Dioxin Assistance," p. 11.

79. "Clean Up Efforts," *The Aspen Institute*, p. 3.

80. Martin, "U.S. Agent Orange/Dioxin Assistance," p. 9.

81. Martin, "U.S. Agent Orange/Dioxin Assistance," p. 12.

82. Martin, "U.S. Agent Orange/Dioxin Assistance," p. 13.

83. Black, "The Lethal Legacy."

84. Program staff (Vietnam Association for Victims of Agent Orange) in discussion with the author, July 2016; Michael F. Martin, "Vietnamese Victims of Agent Orange and U.S.-Vietnam Relations," *Congressional Research Service*, August 29, 2012, accessed July 15, 2016, https://fas.org/sgp/crs/row/RL34761.pdf, p. 27.

85. Program staff (Vietnam Association for Victims of Agent Orange) in discussion with the author, July 2016.

86. "Dealing with the Damage," Agent Orange Record, 2010, accessed June 16, 2016, http://www.agentorangerecord.com/impact_on_vietnam/environment/defoliation/P1, p. 1.

87. Martin, "U.S. Agent Orange/Dioxin Assistance," p. 14.

88. Bailey, "Agent Orange," p. 9.

89. Charles Bailey, "Agent Orange in Vietnam 2012," *The Aspen Institute and Agent Orange in Vietnam Program*, January 28, 2013, accessed

July 22, 2016, https://assets.aspeninstitute.org/content/uploads/files/content/upload/Agent%20Orange%20in%20Vietnam%202012%20Report%20-%20EN.pdf, p. 1.

90. Chuck Searcy (founder of Project RENEW) in discussion with the author, July 2016.

91. Martin, "U.S. Agent Orange/Dioxin Assistance," p. 6.

Chapter 4

1. Louis Maresca, "A New Protocol on Explosive Remnants of War: The History and Negotiation of Protocol V to the 1980 Convention on Certain Conventional Weapons," *Current Issues and Comments, International Committee of the Red Cross*, 86, No. 856 (December 2004), p. 826.

2. The term "High Contracting Parties" refers to states that have signed or ratified a treaty or convention.

3. Danielle Ressler, "A Primer on Explosive Remnants of War," *Journal of Mine Action*, No. 10.1 (2003), accessed September 25, 2016, http://www.jmu.edu/cisr/journal/10.1/feature/ressler/ressler.shtml, p. 6.

4. Maresca, "A New Protocol on Explosive Remnants of War," p. 827.

5. Maresca, "A New Protocol on Explosive Remnants of War," p. 827.

6. Bonnie Docherty, "Breaking New Ground: The Convention on Cluster Munitions and the Evolution of International Humanitarian Law," *Human Rights Quarterly* 31, No.4 (2009), p. 953.

7. Maresca, "A New Protocol on Explosive Remnants of War," p. 830.

8. Katherine Harrison, and Richard Moyes, "Ambiguity in Practice: Benchmarks for the Implementation of CCW Protocol V," *Land Mine Action*. 2009, accessed November 23, 2016, http://www.article36.org/wp-content/uploads/2010/08/ambiguity-in-practice.pdf, p. 30; Maresca, "A New Protocol on Explosive Remnants of War," p. 830.

9. Docherty, "Breaking New Ground," p. 954.

10. Docherty, "Breaking New Ground," p. 954.

11. Docherty, "Breaking New Ground," p. 954. (See also International Law Commission, "Draft Articles of Responsibility for States for Internationally Wrongful Acts with Commentary," *United Nations Yearbook of the International Law Commission*, 2, No. 2, Art. 13 (2001).

12. "The Law of Armed Conflict and the Use of Force." In *The Max Planck Encyclopedia of International Law*, edited by Frauke Lachenmann, and Rudiger Wolfrum (Oxford: Oxford University Press, 2017), p. 1070.

13. Maresca, "A New Protocol on Explosive Remnants of War," p. 827.

14. Yves Sandoz, "Convention of 10 October 1980 on Prohibitions or Restrictions on the Use of Certain Conventional Weapons Which may be Deemed to be Excessively Injurious or to have Indiscriminate Effects (Convention on Certain Conventional Weapons)," *United Nations Audiovisual Library of International Law (Travaux Preparatoires)*, 2010, accessed January 15, 2017, http://legal.un.org/avl/pdf/ha/cprccc/cprccc_e.pdf, p. 3.

15. Sandoz, "Convention of 10 October 1980 on Prohibitions or Restrictions on the Use of Certain Conventional Weapons," p.3.

16. The Convention on Cluster Munitions, accessed on January 15, 2017, http://www.clusterconvention.org, p. 1.

17. Lisa Farrah Ho, "Negotiating the Convention on Cluster Munitions: Lessons Learnt," *Singapore Management University. Accessed January 15, 2017,* http://www.e-ir.info/2014/05/07/negotiating-the-convention-on-cluster-munitions-lessons-learnt, p. 2.

18. The Convention on Cluster Munitions, accessed January 18, 2017, http://www.un.org/en/genocideprevention/documents/atrocity-crimes/Doc.47_conv%20cluster%20munitions.pdf, p. 1.

19. Sandoz, "Convention of 10 October 1980 on Prohibitions or Restrictions on the Use of Certain Conventional Weapons," p. 5.

20. Kevin Riordan, "Convention on Cluster Munitions," *United Nations Audiovisual Library of International Law (Travaux Preparatoires)*, accessed February 10, 2017 http://legal.un.org/avl/ha/ccm/ccm.html, p. 1.

21. Riordan, "Convention on Cluster Munitions," p. 1.

22. Jeff Abramson, "Treaty Analysis: The Convention on Cluster Munitions," *Arms Control Association,* accessed January 25, 2017, https://www.armscontrol.org/act/2008_12/CCM, p. 5.

23. Riordan, "Convention on Cluster Munitions," p. 2.

24. Stephen D. Mull, Assistant Secretary of Political-Military Affairs, "U.S. Cluster Munitions Policy," on-the-record briefing, *United States State Department,* May 2008. Accessed November 6, 2016, https://2001–2009.state.gov/t/pm/rls/rm/105111.htm, p. 1; Megan Burke, "Growing Global Investment in Cluster Munitions Despite International Bans Against Use." *Cluster Munition Coalition,* June 2016. Accessed November 17, 2016, https://www.ngoadvisor.net/cluster-munitions-investment, p. 2.

25. "Cluster Munition Coalition Urges No Use of Cluster Munitions by US and Others in Syria and Iraq," *Cluster Munition Coalition,* September 2014. Accessed October 6, 2016. http://www.stopcluster munitions.org/en-gb/media/news/2014/cluster-munition-coalition-urges-no-use-of-cluster-munitions-by-us-and-others-in-syria-and-iraq.aspx#, p. 1.

26. Sewell Chan, "Report Finds Ban Hasn't Halted Use of Cluster Bombs in Syria or Yemen." Accessed November 6, 2016. https://www.nytimes.com/2016/09/02/world/middleeast/cluster-bombs-syria-yemen.html?_r=0, p. 2.

27. Chan, "Report Finds Ban Hasn't Halted Use of Cluster Bombs in Syria or Yemen," p. 2.

28. Mull, *United States State Department*, p. 1.

29. 1925 Geneva Protocol: Protocol for the Prohibition of the Use in War of Asphyxiating, Poisonous, or Other Gases, and of Other Bacteriological Methods of Warfare, Geneva, 17, June 1925, accessed January 19, 2017, https://unoda-web.s3-accelerate.amazonaws.com/wp-content/uploads/assets/WMD/Bio/pdf/Status_Protocol.pdf, p. 1.

30. United Nations, "Convention on the Prohibition of Military or Any Other Hostile Use of Environmental Modification Techniques," accessed February 10, 2017, http://www.un-documents.net/enmod. htm, p. 1.

31. United Nations Office for Disarmament Affairs, "Convention on the Prohibition of Military or Any Other Hostile Use of Environmental Modification Techniques," https://www.un.org/disarmament/geneva/enmod, p. 1.

32. Antoine Bouvier, "Protection of the Natural Environment in Time of Armed Conflict," *International Review of the Red Cross* 285 (1991), accessed February 10, 2017, https://www.icrc.org/eng/resources/documents/article/other/57jmau.htm, p. 1.

33. United States Department of State, Office of the Historian, Bureau of Public Affairs: 199. Memorandum from David Elliott of the National Security Council Staff to the President's Assistant for National Security Affairs (Scowcroft), accessed February 12, 2017, https://history.state.gov/historicaldocuments/frus1969-76ve14p2/d199, p. 1.

34. Australian Defense Headquarters Publication 06.4, 4.11 and 7.17. *The Manual of the Law of Armed Conflict,* May 11, 2006. Accessed January 22, 2016. https://ihl-databases.icrc.org/customary-ihl/eng/docs/v2_rul_rule76, p. 1.

35. "Practice Relating to Rule 76. Herbicides," *International Committee of the Red Cross.* Accessed December 14, 2016. https://ihl-databases. icrc.org/customary-ihl/eng/docs/v2_rul_rule76, p. 1.

36. United States Court of Appeals for the Second Circuit, *Vietnam Association for Victims of Agent Orange, et al v. Dow Chemical Company, et al,* Judgment, February 22, 2001. Accessed February 14, 2017, https://www.state.gov/documents/organization/98481.pdf, p. 8.

37. United States Department of State, *Bureau of International Security and Nonproliferation, Convention on the Prohibition of Military or Any Other Hostile Use of Environmental Modification Techniques: Understandings Regarding the Convention: Understandings Relating to Article I, paragraph. C,* accessed on February 14, 2017, https://www.state.gov/t/isn/4783.htm#understandings, p. 1.

38. Antoine Bouvier, "Recent Studies on the Protection of the Environment in Time of Armed Conflict," *International Review of the Red Cross,* 32, No. 291 (1992), p. 554.

39. U.S. Department of State, "Convention on the Prohibition of Military or Any Other Hostile Use of Environmental Modification Techniques," accessed February 3, 2016. https://www.state.gov/t/isn/4783.htm, p. 6.

40. "Practice Relating to Rule 76. Herbicides," *International Committee of the Red Cross,* p. 1.

41. "Protecting the Environment During Armed Conflict: An Inventory and Analysis of International Law," *United Nations Environmental Program* (2009), accessed December 10, 2016. http://www.un.org/zh/events/environmentconflictday/pdfs/int_law.pdf, p. 12.

42. "Environmental Remediation," USAID, accessed February 10, 2017, https://www.usaid.gov/vietnam/environmental-remediation, p. 1.

43. "Genesis and Historical Development," Organization for the Prohibition of Chemical Weapons (OPCW), accessed February 10, 2017, https://www.opcw.org/chemical-weapons-convention/genesis-and-historical-development, p. 2.

44. Chemical Weapons Convention, Article 1.

45. Ibid, Article 1 (c).

46. Ibid, Article 10.

47. Ibid, Article 2 (1)(a).

48. Ibid, Article 2 (2).

49. "Brief Description of Chemical Weapons," Organization for the Prohibition of Chemical Weapons, accessed February 10, 2017, https://www.opcw.org/about-chemical-weapons/what-is-a-chemical-weapon, p. 2.

50. "IARC Monographs on the Evaluation of Carcinogenic Risks to Humans," Polychlorinated Dibenzo-para-Dioxins and Polychlorinated Dibenzofurans, Volume 69, *World Health Organization International Agency for Research on Cancer.*

51. Chemical Weapons Convention, Article 1 (3).

52. Ibid, Article 2 (6).

53. Ibid, Article 2 (8).

54. USAID. "Environmental Remediation." 2017. https://www.usaid.gov/vietnam/environmental-remediation.

55. Ibid, Articles 4 (16) and Article 5 (19).

56. 1925 Geneva Protocol, p. 1.

57. United Nations GAOR, Res. 2603-A, 24th Session, "Question of chemical and bacteriological (biological) weapons," December 16, 1969, p. 9.

58. Convention on Chemical Weapons, Article 1 (3).

59. Ibid, Article 2 (6).

60. Ibid, Article 2 (8).

Chapter 5

1. The Statute of the International Court of Justice acknowledges customary international law in Article 38(1)(b); and it is also incorporated into Article 92 of the United Nations Charter.

2. The Statute of the International Court of Justice, Article 38(1)(b).

3. Thomas Buergenthal and Sean D. Murphy, *Public International Law in a Nutshell, 5th edition,* (St. Paul: West Academic Publishing, 2013), p. 28; Yoram Dinstein, *The Conduct of Hostilities Under the Law of International Armed Conflict,* (Cambridge: Cambridge University Press, 2004), p. 5.

4. Buergenthal and Murphy, p. 28.

5. Ibid, p. 27.

6. Ibid, p. 28.

7. Susan Notar, "General Principles of International Law: Customary International Law," *International Judicial Monitor,* 1, No. 5. (2006), accessed February 17, 2017, http://www.judicialmonitor.org/archive_1206/generalprinciples.html, p. 1.

8. Shabtai Rosenne, *Practice and Methods of International Law,* (New York: Oceana Publications Inc., 1984), p. 55; International Court of Justice, *United Kingdom v. Norway,* 1951.

9. Michael P. Scharf, "Accelerated Formation of Customary International Law," *Case Western Reserve University School of Law, Faculty Publications* (2014), p. 309.

10. "Customary International Humanitarian Law," *International Committee of the Red Cross.* Accessed March 10, 2016. https://www.icrc.org/en/document/customary-international-humanitarian-law-0, p. 1.

11. Scharf, "Accelerated Formation," p. 309.

12. Ibid, p. 309.

13. Ibid, 309.

14. Farhad Talaie, "The Importance of Custom and the Process of Formation in Modern International Law," *James Cook University Law Review* (1998), p. 35.

15. Buergenthal and Murphy, p. 28.

16. Majid Khadduri, as quoted in Peter Malanczuk's *Modern Introduction to International Law, 7ᵗʰ edition* (New York: Routledge, 1997), p. 9.

17. Andre da Rocha Ferreira et al. "Formation and Evidence of Customary International Law," *International Law Commission, Model United Nations Journal,* 1 (2013), p. 183.

18. Ibid, p. 183.

19. Convention with Respect to the Laws and Customs of War on Land (Hague, II), July 29, 1899, Section III, Article 43. Yale Law School. Accessed March 12, 2016. http://avalon.law.yale.edu/19th_century/hague02.asp, p. 7.

20. Convention (IV) respecting the Laws and Customs of War on Land and its annex: Regulations concerning the Laws and Customs of War on Land, The Hague, October 18, 1907, *International Committee of the Red Cross.* Accessed August 14, 2016. https://ihl-databases.icrc.org/ihl/INTRO/195, p. 1.

21. Ibid, p. 1.

22. Ibid, Article 231 and 232.

23. Ibid, Article 232.

24. Treaty of Versailles, Article 232.

25. "Customary International Law," *International Judicial Monitor* 1, no. 5 (2006). Accessed January 7, 2017. http://www.judicialmonitor.org/archive_1206/generalprinciples.html, p. 1.

26. Vienna Convention on the Law of Treaties. *United States Department of State.* https://www.state.gov/s/l/treaty/faqs/70139.htm, p.1.

27. The full name of the 1925 Geneva Protocol is "The 1925 Geneva Protocol for the Prohibition of the Use in War of Asphyxiating,

Poisonous or other Gases, and of Bacteriological Methods of Warfare."

28. Richard A. Falk, *The Vietnam War and International Law Volume 4: The Concluding Phase.* (Princeton: Princeton University Press, 1976), p. 201.

29. Angela Woodward, "The 1925 Geneva Protocol Goes Digital," *VERTIC Blog*, May 17, 2012. Accessed November 16, 2017. http://www.vertic.org/pages/posts/the-1925-geneva-protocol-goes-digital-298.php, p. 1.

30. Jeanne Stellman et al, "The Extent and Patterns of Usage of Agent Orange and Other Herbicides in Vietnam." *Nature* 422 (April 17, 2003), p. 685.

31. "Public Appeal of International Lawyers Concerning the Responsibility of the United States Toward Vietnam for the Sprayings of Agent Orange/Dioxin," Press release of Initial Endorsers, April 29, 2007, p. 2.

32. Cleanup requirements exist in each of the following conventions: Convention on Environmental Modification (1977); Convention on Chemical Weapons (1977); Convention on Certain Conventional Weapons (2006); and Convention on Custer Munitions (2010).

33. Paris Peace Accords, Article 21, 1973.

34. "Reparations," The International Center for Transitional Justice. Accessed December 13, 2016. https://www.ictj.org/our-work/transitional-justice-issues/reparations, p. 1.

35. Ibid, p. 1.

36. "What is Reparation?" REDRESS. Accessed December 13, 2016. www.redress.org/what-is-reparation/what-is-reparation, p. 1.

37. "Basic Principles and Guidelines on the Right to a Remedy and Reparation for Victims of Gross Violations of International Human Rights Law and Serious Violations of International

Humanitarian Law," *United Nations Human Rights Office of the High Commissioner.* Accessed September 14, 2016. www.ohchr.org/en/professionalinterest/pages/remedyandreparation.aspx, p. 1.

38. Including the International Covenant on Civil and Political Rights (Article 2); the International Convention on the Elimination of All Forms of Racial Discrimination (Article 6); the Convention Against Torture (Article 140); the Convention on the Rights of the Child (Article 39).

39. Including resolutions and guidelines adopted by the U.S. General Assembly; The Hague Convention IV Respecting the Laws and Customs of War on Land (Article 3); the Universal Declaration of Human Rights (Article 8); the Geneva Conventions Additional Protocol I Relating to the Protection of Victims of International Armed Conflicts (Article 91); the Rome Statue of the International Criminal Court (Articles 75 and 78).

40. Permanent Court of Arbitration, Chorzow Factory Case (Ger. V. Pol.), PCIJ, Sr. A. No. at 29.

41. Ibid.

42. Andrew Childers and Anna Lamut, "Legal Foundations for 'Making Amends' to Civilians Harmed by Armed Conflict." *Harvard Law School International Human Rights Clinic* (2012), p. 2.

43. Pablo De Greiff, *The Handbook on Reparations,* (Oxford: Oxford University Press, 2006).

44. Childers and Lamut, p. 2.

45. REDRESS, p. 2; *United Nations Human Rights Office of the High Commissioner* p. 5.

46. The notion of respecting, protecting and fulfilling rights is also referred to as "realizing rights." Respect (refrain from interfering with established rights); protect (prevent against abuses by non-state actors), and fulfill (actively safeguard and enforce rights).

47. "Customary IHL: Role 150. Reparation," *International Committee of the Red Cross*. Accessed February 22, 2016. https://ihl-databases.icrc.org/customary-ihl/eng/docs/v1_rul_rule150.

48. "Customary IHL: Role 150. Reparation," *International Committee of the Red Cross*.

49. Chorzow Factory Case (cited in The Law I, § 73). See also PCIJ Statute, Article 36, which states that "the States Parties to the present Statute may at any time declare that they recognize as compulsory *ipso facto* and without special agreement, in relation to any other state accepting the same obligation, the jurisdiction of the Court in all legal disputes concerning: … (d) the nature or extent of the reparation to be made for the breach of an international obligation." Article 36 of the ICJ Statute contains similar wording.

50. The Islah Reparations Project lists additional examples of reparations initiatives, accessed February 15, 2016. http://www.reparations.org/why-reparations/history-of-reparations, p. 1–3. (See also REDRESS http://www.redress.org/key-cases/key-cases, and the International Center for Transitional Justice, accessed February 15, 2016, https://www.ictj.org/our-work/transitional-justice-issues/reparations. p. 3–4.)

51. Childers and Lamut, p. 3.

52. Ibid, p. 7.

53. Ibid, p. 7.

54. Legal definition of reparation: http://legal-dictionary.thefreedictionary.com/reparation. Accessed January 4, 2016.

55. The first class-action lawsuit filed by a U.S. veteran about the damages caused by Agent Orange occurred in 1978. Paul Reutershan, a twenty-eight-year-old veteran, believed that his chloracne and abdominal cancer were related to exposure to Agent Orange. He sued chemical manufacturers including Dow and Monsanto, and

in 1978 (after Reutershan's death), monetary compensation of $330 million ($150 million more than the original $180 million due to invested assets) was distributed to Class members. (See Agent Orange Record: http://wwww.agentorangerecord.com/information/the_quest_for_additional_relief/. Accessed August 20, 2016.)

56. Chorzow Factory Case.

57. Bonnie Docherty, "Breaking New Ground: The Convention on Cluster Munitions and the Evolution of International Humanitarian Law," *Human Rights Quarterly* 31, no. 4 (2009), p. 935.

Chapter 7

1. "Landmine Monitor 2016, Contamination and Clearance." *Landmine and Cluster Munition Monitor*. 2016. http://the-monitor.org/en-gb/reports/2016/landmine-monitor-2016/contamination-and-clearance.aspx. p. 1.

2. "International Human Rights Instruments. Report on Reservations." United Nations. Seventh Inter-Committee Meeting of the Human Rights Treaty Bodies. Accessed July 27, 2016. www2.ohchr.org/english/bodies/icm-mc/docs/hri.mc.2008.5.doc.

3. "The Failure of the United States to Comply with the Convention Against Torture." American Civil Liberties Union. p. 14. Accessed July 27, 2016. https://www.aclu.org/files/safefree/torture/A.pdf.

4. "The Failure of the United States to Comply with the Convention Against Torture." American Civil Liberties Union. p. 14. Accessed January 16, 2016. https://www.aclu.org/files/safefree/torture/A.pdf.

5. State Party (also States Parties) is defined by the United Nations as a country that has ratified or acceded to a particular treaty and is therefore legally bound by the provisions in said instrument.

6. U.S. Department of State. Accessed July 6, 2016. https://www.state.gov/s/l/treaty/faqs/70139.htm

7. The UN lists 9 major human rights treaties in addition to the Universal Declaration of Human Rights: http://www.ohchr.org/EN/ProfessionalInterest/Pages/CoreInstruments.aspx. Accessed March 10, 2016.

8. Sifa Mtango. "A State of Oppression? Women's Rights in Saudi Arabia." *Asia-Pacific Journal on Human Rights and the Law.* 1 (2004): 49–67; Human Rights Watch. "Perpetual Minors: Human Rights Abuses Stemming from Male Guardianship and Sex Segregation in Saudi Arabia." 2008. 1–53.

9. *The Persistent Power of Human Rights From Commitment to Compliance.* Edited by Thomas Risse, Stephen C. Ropp, Kathryn Sikkink (Cambridge: Cambridge University Press, 2013). It is to be noted that these authors were among the first to use quantitative and qualitative research and theory to address and analyze the various causal mechanisms and conditions, which produce compliance, as well as violations, among states in regards to human rights.

10. *The Persistent Power of Human Rights From Commitment to Compliance.* Edited by Thomas Risse, Stephen C. Ropp, Kathryn Sikkink (Cambridge: Cambridge University Press, 2013).

11. *The Persistent Power of Human Rights From Commitment to Compliance.* Edited by Thomas Risse, Stephen C. Ropp, Kathryn Sikkink (Cambridge: Cambridge University Press, 2013).

12. *The Persistent Power of Human Rights From Commitment to Compliance.* Edited by Thomas Risse, Stephen C. Ropp, Kathryn Sikkink (Cambridge: Cambridge University Press, 2013).

13. The author in conversation with John G. (Jack) Healey, July 12, 2017.

References

Abramson, Jeff. "Treaty Analysis: The Convention on Cluster Munitions." *Arms Control Association.* Accessed January 25, 2017. https://www.armscontrol.org/act/2008_12/CCM.

"Agent Orange." *The American Public Health Association.* Accessed July 7, 2016. https://www.apha.org/policies-and-advocacy/public-health-policy-statements/policy-database/2014/07/29/13/22/agent-orange.

"Agent Orange's Shameful Legacy." *The Week.* Accessed July 6, 2016. http://theweek.com/articles/472668/agent-oranges-shameful-legacy.

"All You Ever Wanted to Know About Dioxin or Perhaps You Really Do Not Want to Know." *Agent Orange Association of Canada.* Accessed July 19, 2016. http://www.agentorangecanada.com/dioxin.php.

Australian Defense Headquarters. *Publication 06.4, 4.11 and 7.17: The Manual of the Law of Armed Conflict.* Accessed February 12, 2017.

Bailey, Charles. "Agent Orange in Vietnam 2012." *The Aspen Institute and Agent Orange in Vietnam Program.* Accessed July 22, 2016, https://assets.aspeninstitute.org/content/uploads/files/content/upload/Agent%20Orange%20in%20Vietnam%202012%20Report%20-%20EN.pdf.

Bailey, Charles. "Agent Orange: What Efforts Are Being Made to Address the Continuing Impact of Dioxin in Vietnam?" Written testimony prepared for The House Committee on Foreign Affairs Subcommittee on Asia the Pacific and the Global Environment, Washington, DC, June 2009.

Bailey, Charles, and Susan Hammond, "Frequently Asked Questions About Agent Orange/Dioxin." *War Legacies Project and Ford Foundation.* Accessed June 9, 2016, http://www.agentorangerecord.com/images/uploads/modules/AODFAQ.pdf.

"Basic Principles and Guidelines on the Right to a Remedy and Reparation for Victims of Gross Violations of International Human Rights Law and Serious Violations of International Humanitarian Law." *United Nations Human Rights Office of the High Commissioner.* www.ohchr.org/en/professionalinterest/pages/remedyandreparation.aspx.

Black, George. "The Lethal Legacy of the Vietnam War." *The Nation.* March 16, 2015 https://www.thenation.com/article/lethal-legacy-vietnam-war.

Black, George. "The Vietnam War is Still Killing People." *The New Yorker.* May 20, 2016. http://www.newyorker.com/news/news-desk/the-vietnam-war-is-still-killing-people.

Bouvier, Antoine. "Protection of the Natural Environment in Time of Armed Conflict. "*International Review of the Red Cross.* Accessed February 10, 2017. https://www.icrc.org/eng/resources/documents/article/other/57jmau.htm.

Bouvier, Antoine. "Recent Studies on the Protection of the Environment in Time of Armed Conflict." *International Review of the Red Cross* 32, no. 291 (1992): 554-566.

Buergenthal, Thomas and Sean D. Murphy. *Public International Law in a Nutshell, 5th edition.* St. Paul: West Academic Publishing, 2013.

Bunn, George. "Banning Poison Gas and Germ Warfare: Should the United States Agree?" *Wisconsin Law Review* 1949, no. 375 (1969): 375–420.

Butler, Declan. "Flight Records Reveal Full Extent of Agent Orange Contamination in Vietnam." *Nature* 422, no. 6933 (2003). Accessed June 11, 2016. http://www.nature.com/news/2003/030417/full/news030414-10.html.

Chau, Beyond the Lines. Directed by Courtney Marsh. United States: Seventh Art Releasing, 2015.

Childers, Andrew and Anna Lamut. "Legal Foundations for 'Making Amends' to Civilians Harmed by Armed Conflict." *Harvard Law School International Human Rights Clinic* (2012): 2–14.

Chorzow Factory Case (Ger. V. Pol.), 1997, PCIJ, Sr. A. No. 9. Permanent Court of Arbitration. Accessed February 21, 2017. http://www.worldcourts.com/pcij/eng/decisions/1927.07.26_chorzow.htm.

Chuck Searcy (Founder of Project RENEW) in discussion with the author, July, 2016.

Chuck Searcy, "U.S. Veteran Leads Clean-up of Vietnam War's Lethal Remnants," *PBS Newshour.* November 20, 2014. http://www.pbs.org/newshour/bb/u-s-veteran-leads-clean-vietnam-wars-lethal-remnants

"Clean Up Efforts." *The Aspen Institute.* Accessed July 10, 2016. https://www.aspeninstitute.org/programs/agent-orange-in-vietnam-program/cleaning-up-contaminated-soil.

Clodfelter, Michael. *Vietnam in Military Statistics: A History of the Indochina Wars 1772 –1991.* Jefferson: McFarland and Company, Inc., 1995.

"Cluster Bomb Fact Sheet." Legacies of War. http://legaciesofwar.org/resources/cluster-bomb-fact-sheet.

"Cluster Bombs," *Handicap International United Kingdom.* Accessed July 10, 2016. http://www.handicap-international.us/cluster_bombs.

Cohn, Marjorie. "Agent Orange: Terrible Legacy of the Vietnam War." Thomas Jefferson School of Law. *The Huffington Post.* May 1, 2016. http://www.huffingtonpost.com/marjorie-cohn/agent-orange-terrible-legacy_b_7189938.html.

Cunningham, Chloe. "U.S. and Vietnam Sign Memorandum of Understanding." *The Journal of ERW and Mine Action* 18, no. 1 (2014): 6.

"Customary IHL: Practice Relating to Rule 76: Herbicides." *International Committee of the Red Cross.* https://ihl-databases.icrc.org/customary-ihl/eng/docs/v2_rul_rule76.

"Customary IHL: Role 150. Reparation." *International Committee of the Red Cross.* Accessed February 21, 2017. https://ihl-databases.icrc.org/customary-ihl/eng/docs/v1_rul_rule150.

Czaplinkski, Wladyslaw. "Jus Cogens and the Law of Treaties." In Tomuschat, Christian and Jean-Marc Thouvenin, *The Fundamental Rules of the International Legal Order.* The Netherlands: Brill-Nijhoff, 2005.

da Rocha Ferreira, Andre et al. "Formation and Evidence of Customary International Law." *International Law Commission, Model United Nations Journal* 1 (2013): 182–201.

Dang Duc Nhu et al. "A GIS Study of Dioxin Contamination in a Vietnamese Region Sprayed with Herbicide." *Environmental Health and Preventive Medicine* 14, no. 6 (2009): 353–360.

De Greiff, Pablo. *The Handbook on Reparations.* Oxford: Oxford University Press, 2006.

"Dealing with the Damage." *Agent Orange Record.* Accessed June 16, 2016. http://www.agentorangerecord.com/impact_on_vietnam/environment/defoliation/P1.

Dinstein, Yoram. *The Conduct of Hostilities Under the Law of International Armed Conflict.* Cambridge: Cambridge University Press, 2004.

"Dioxins and Their Effects on Human Health." *World Health Organization.* Accessed July 8, 2016. http://www.who.int/mediacentre/factsheets/fs225/en.

Docherty, Bonnie. "Breaking New Ground: The Convention on Cluster Munitions and the Evolution of International Humanitarian Law." *Human Rights Quarterly* 31, no.4 (2009): 954–963. http://hrp.law.harvard.edu/wp-content/uploads/2013/08/31.4.docherty.pdf.

"Eating, Drinking, Touching, Breathing, Nursing, Conceiving." *Agent Orange Record.* Accessed June 10, 2016. http://www.agentorangerecord. com/impact_on_vietnam/health.

Edward A. Laws, *Aquatic Pollution: An Introductory Text.* 3rd edition. Los Angeles: John Wiley & Sons, 2000.

Falk, Richard A. *The Vietnam War and International Law Volume 4: The Concluding Phase.* Princeton: Princeton University Press, 1976.

"Ford Foundation's Landmark Work on Agent Orange Transitions to Aspen Institute." *The Ford Foundation.* May 5, 2011. Accessed June 22, 2016. http://www.fordfoundation.org/the-latest/news/ford-foundations-landmark-work-on-agent-orange-transitions-to-aspen-institute.

Gumbo, Judy. *The People Make the Peace: Lessons from the Vietnam Antiwar Movement.* Edited by Karín Aguilar-San Juan and Frank Joyce. Charlottesville: Just World Books, 2015.

Guthrie, Jonathon, and Portia Stratton. "The Quang Tri Integrated Survey and Clearance Project." *The Journal of ERW and Mine Action* 19, no. 1 (2015): 16–18.

Hamel, Brant. "Dioxin Exposure Causes Transgenerational Health Effects." The National Institute of Environmental Health Sciences 120, no. 11 (2012): 55—56. Accessed July 19, 2016. https://www.niehs.nih.gov/ news/newsletter/2012/11/file166803_alt.pdf.

Hamilton, Martha. "First of Monsanto Workers' Agent Orange Trials Is Set." *The Washington Post.* Accessed July 15, 2016. https://www. washingtonpost.com/archive/business/1984/06/10/first-of-monsanto-workers-agent-orange-trials-is-set/52f2d640-d050-4325-a939-2043a937830f/?utm_term=.b26b837418dc.

"Hard To Clear Post-war Bombs and Mines." *Vietnam Government Portal Online Newspaper of the Government.* May 14, 2014. http://news. chinhphu.vn/Home/Hard-to-clear-postwar-bombs-and-mines/20125/ 14389.vgp.

Harrison, James P. *The Vietnam War: Vietnamese and American Perspectives.* Edited by Jayne S. Werner and Luu Doan Huynh. Armonk: M.E. Sharpe, 1993.

Harrison, Katherine, and Richard Moyes. "Ambiguity in Practice: Benchmarks for the Implementation of CCW Protocol V." *Land Mine Action.* Accessed November 23, 2016. http://www.article36.org/wp-content/uploads/2010/08/ambiguity-in-practice.pdf.

Hatfield Consultants, Ltd. "Preliminary Assessment of Environmental Impacts Related to Spraying of Agent Orange Herbicide During the Viet Nam War." Accessed July 11, 2016. http://www.hatfieldgroup.com/wp-content/uploads/AgentOrangeReports/CIDA614/default.htm.

"Health Effects." *The Aspen Institute.* 2011. https://www.aspeninstitute.org/programs/agent-orange-in-vietnam-program/health-effects.

Hirschman, Charles et al., "Vietnamese Casualties During the American War: A New Estimate." Population and Development Review 21, no. 4 (1995): 783–812. Accessed June 12, 2016. https://faculty.washington.edu/charles/new%20PUBS/A77.pdf.

Ho, Lisa Farrah. "Negotiating the Convention on Cluster Munitions: Lessons Learnt." *Singapore Management University.* Accessed January 14, 2017. http://www.e-ir.info/2014/05/07/negotiating-the-convention-on-cluster-munitions-lessons-learnt.

Hostetter, Doug. *The People Make the Peace: Lessons from the Vietnam Antiwar Movement.* Edited by Karín Aguilar-San Juan and Frank Joyce. Charlottesville: Just World Books, 2015.

"Hot Spots: Cleaning Up Dioxin-Contaminated Soils." *The Aspen Institute.* Accessed July 10, 2016. https://assets.aspeninstitute.org/content/uploads/files/content/docs/agent-orange/4AOVIIFactSheet-HotSpots-CleaningUpDioxin-ContaminatedSoils-Aug2011.pdf.

Human Rights Watch and Harvard Law School International Human Rights Clinic. "Convention on Cluster Munitions: Q&A on Interoperability and the Prohibition on Assistance." *Human Rights*

Watch. Accessed on January 15, 2017. https://www.hrw.org/sites/default/files/related_material/Convention%20on%20Cluster%20Munitions%20-%20Q%26A%20on%20Interoperability%20and%20the%20Prohibition%20on%20Assistance.pdf.

Interactions with a Violent Past: Reading Post-Conflict Landscapes in Cambodia, Laos, and Vietnam. Edited by Vatthana Pholsena and Oliver Tappe. Singapore: National University of Singapore, Press. 2013.

International Committee of the Red Cross. "Explosive Remnants of War." *International Committee of the Red Cross Resource Center.* 2014.

International Court of Justice, *United Kingdom v. Norway,* 1951.

International Law Association. London Conference, Committee on Formation of Customary (General) International Law, 2000.

International Law Commission. "Draft Articles of Responsibility for States for Internationally Wrongful Acts with Commentary." *United Nations Yearbook of the International Law Commission* 2, no. 2 (2001): 31–143. http://legal.un.org/ilc/texts/instruments/english/commentaries/9_6_2001.pdf.

Johansson, Annika, and Le Thi Nham Tuyet. "Impact of Chemical Warfare with Agent Orange on Women's Reproductive Lives in Vietnam: A Pilot Study." *Reproductive Health Matters* 9, no. 18 (2001): 156–164.

Kiernan, Ben, and Taylor Owen. "Making More Enemies than We Kill? Calculating U.S. Bomb Tonnages Dropped on Laos and Cambodia, and Weighing Their Implications." *Japan Focus: The Asia-Pacific Journal* 13, no. 16.3 (2015).

Kolko, Gabriel. *Anatomy of a War: Vietnam, the United States, and the Modern Historical Experience.* New York: Pantheon Books, 1985.

Lewy, Guenter. *America in Vietnam.* Oxford: Oxford University Press, 1978.

MacPherson, Myra. *The People Make the Peace: Lessons from the Vietnam Antiwar Movement.* Edited by Karín Aguilar-San Juan and Frank Joyce. Charlottesville: Just World Books, 2015.

Malanczuk, Peter. *Modern Introduction to International Law, 7th edition*. New York: Routledge, 1997.

Maresca, Louis. "A New Protocol on Explosive Remnants of War: The History and Negotiation of Protocol V to the 1980 Convention on Certain Conventional Weapons." *Current Issues and Comments, International Committee of the Red Cross* 86, no. 856 (2004): 815 – 835. https://www.icrc.org/eng/assets/files/other/irrc_856_maresca.pdf.

Martin, Michael F. "U.S. Agent Orange/Dioxin Assistance to Vietnam." *Congressional Research Service*. Accessed July 20, 2016. https://fas.org/sgp/crs/row/R44268.pdf.

Monographs on the Evaluation of Carcinogenic Risks to Humans. "Polychlorinated dibenzo-para-dioxins and polychlorinated dibenzofurans." *World Health Organization International Agency for Research on Cancer*. Accessed February 7, 2017. http://monographs.iarc.fr/ENG/Monographs/vol69/mono69.pdf.

National Archives, *Military Records: Statistical Information About Fatal Casualties of the Vietnam War*. 2008. http://www.archives.gov/research/military/vietnam-war/casualty-statistics.html.

Ngo Xuan Hien, and Nguyen Thanh Phu (Project RENEW staff) in discussion with the author, July, 2016.

Notar, Susan. "General Principles of International Law: Customary International Law." *International Judicial Monitor* 1, No. 5 (2006).

Olson, Wyatt. "A New Approach to Ridding Vietnam of Unexploded Ordnance." *Stars and Stripes*. May 6, 2012. https://www.stripes.com/news/pacific/a-new-approach-to-ridding-vietnam-of-unexploded-ordnance-1.176497#.WOUaMWe1vIU.

Organization for Economic Co-operation and Development. "Conflict, Peace-Building, Disarmament, Security: Gender Perspectives on Landmines." *The United Nations Department for Disarmament Affairs*. Accessed June 10, 2016. http://www.oecd.org/social/gender-development/1896552.pdf.

Organization for the Prohibition of Chemical Weapons (OPCW): *Genesis and Historical Development.* https://www.opcw.org/chemical-weapons-convention/genesis-and-historical-development.

Program staff (Vietnam Association for Victims of Agent Orange) in discussion with the author, July, 2016.

Program staff (Vietnam Women's Union) in discussion with the author, July, 2016.

Project RENEW. http://landmines.org.vn.

"Promoting Hope and Dignity: A Long-Term Humanitarian Response to Agent Orange and Dioxin in Vietnam," *The Aspen Institute.* Accessed July 11, 2016. https://www.aspeninstitute.org/programs/agent-orange-in-vietnam-program/promoting-hope-dignity-long-term-humanitarian-response-agent-orange-dioxin-vietnam.

"Protecting the Environment During Armed Conflict: An Inventory and Analysis of International Law." *United Nations Environmental Program* (2009). http://www.un.org/zh/events/environmentconflictday/pdfs/int_law.pdf.

"Public Appeal of International Lawyers Concerning the Responsibility of the United States Toward Vietnam for the Sprayings of Agent Orange/Dioxin." Press release of Initial Endorsers. April 29, 2007. http://docplayer.net/32005409-Public-appeal-of-international-lawyers-concerning-the-responsibility-of-the-united-states-toward-vietnam-for-the-sprayings-of-agent-orange-dioxin.html.

Quang Tri Province Legacy of War Coordination Center (LWCC). Accessed June 14, 2016. http://lwcc-dbu-quangtri.vn/en-us/Home.

"Reparations." The International Center for Transitional Justice. Accessed February 17, 2017. https://www.ictj.org/our-work/transitional-justice-issues/reparations.

Ressler, Danielle. "A Primer on Explosive Remnants of War." *Journal of Mine Action* no. 10.1 (2003). http://www.jmu.edu/cisr/journal/10.1/feature/ressler/ressler.shtml.

Rosenne, Shabtai. *Practice and Methods of International Law*. New York: Oceana Publications Inc., 1984.

Sandoz, Yves. "Convention of 10 October 1980 on Prohibitions or Restrictions on the Use of Certain Conventional Weapons Which may be Deemed to be Excessively Injurious or to have Indiscriminate Effects (Convention on Certain Conventional Weapons)." *United Nations Audiovisual Library of International Law (Travaux Preparatoires)*. Acessed January 15, 2017, http://legal.un.org/avl/pdf/ha/cprccc/cprccc_e.pdf.

Scharf, Michael P. "Accelerated Formation of Customary International Law." *Case Western Reserve University School of Law, Faculty Publications* (2014): 306–342.

Schecter, Arnold. "Statement to the House Subcommittee on Asia, the Pacific and the Global Environment on the impact of Agent Orange." Vietnam Agent Orange Relief and Responsibility Campaign, Washington, DC, May 2008.

Schecter, Arnold, et al. "Recent Dioxin Contamination From Agent Orange in Residents of a Southern Vietnam City." *Journal of Occupational and Environmental Medicine* 43, no. 5 (2001): 435-443.

Searcy, Chuck. (Founder of Project RENEW) in discussion with the author, July, 2016.

Sirleaf, Ellen Johnson, and Elisabeth Rehn. *Women, War, Peace and Landmines*. New York: United Nations Development Fund for Women. 2004.

"Spillover." *Agent Orange Record*. Accessed June 22, 2016. http://www.agentorangerecord.com/impact_on_vietnam/environment/hot_spots.

Stapleton, John. *Agent Orange: The Cleanup Begins*. Sydney: A Sense of Place Publishing, Inc. 2013.

Stellman, Jeanne. "The Extent and Patterns of Usage of Agent Orange and Other Herbicides in Vietnam." *Nature* 422 (2003).

Talaie, Farhad. "The Importance of Custom and the Process of Formation in Modern International Law." *James Cook University Law Review* (1998): 27–45.

"The Chemical Scythe." *Agent Orange Record.* Accessed July 15, 2016. http://www.agentorangerecord.com/impact_on_vietnam/environment/defoliation.

The Encyclopedia of the Vietnam War: A Political, Social, and Military History. 5th edition. Edited by Dr. Spencer Tucker and Dr. Paul G. Pierpaoli Jr. Santa Barbara, California: ABC-CLIO, 2011.

"The Invisible Enemy." *Agent Orange Record.* Accessed July 1, 2016. http://www.agentorangerecord.com/agent_orange_history/in_vietnam.

The Islah Reparations Project. http://www.reparations.org/why-reparations/history-of-reparations.

"The Law of Armed Conflict and the Use of Force." In *The Max Planck Encyclopedia of International Law*, edited by Frauke Lachenmann and Rudiger Wolfrum. Oxford: Oxford University Press, 2017.

Tran Thi Tuyet-Hanh, et al. "Environmental Health Risk Assessment of Dioxin Exposure Through Foods in a Dioxin Hot Spot—Bien Hoa City, Vietnam." *International Journal of Environmental Research and Public Health* 7, no. 5 (2010): 2398–2406. https://www.ncbi.nlm.nih.gov/pmc/articles/PMC2898056/pdf/ijerph-07-02395.pdf.

"U.S. Pledges $90 Million to Clear Unexploded Ordnance in Laos." *TIME Magazine,* September 5, 2016. http://time.com/4479692/u-s-pledges-90-million-to-clear-unexploded-ordinances-in-Laos.

United Nations GAOR, Res. 2603-A, 24th Session, "Question of Chemical and Bacteriological (biological) Weapons." December 16, 1969.

United States Court of Appeals for the Second Circuit. *Vietnam Association for Victims of Agent Orange, et al v. Dow Chemical Company, et al.* Accessed February 14, 2017, https://www.state.gov/documents/organization/98481.pdf.

United States Department of Defense. "Principal Wars in Which the United States Participated –U.S. Military Personnel Serving and Casualties." *Defense Casuality Analysis System.* Accessed June 11, 2016, https://www.dmdc.osd.mil/dcas/pages/report_principal_wars.xhtml.

United States Department of State. *Bureau of International Security and Nonproliferation, Convention on the Prohibition of Military or Any Other Hostile Use of Environmental Modification Techniques: Understandings Regarding the Convention: Understandings Relating to Article I, paragraph. C.* Accessed on February 14, 2017. https://www.state.gov/t/isn/4783.htm#understandings.

United States Department of State. *Office of the Historian, Bureau of Public Affairs: 199. Memorandum from David Elliott of the National Security Council Staff to the President's Assistant for National Security Affairs (Scowcroft).* Accessed February 12, 2017. https://history.state.gov/historicaldocuments/frus1969-76ve14p2/d199.

USAID. *Environmental Remediation.* https://www.usaid.gov/vietnam/environmental-remediation.

Waldeck, Wendy, and Sarah Sensamaust. "Vietnam." *Journal of Mine Action* 9, no. 2 (2006).

War Remnants Museum, Ho Chi Minh City, Vietnam.

Wells-Dang, Andrew. "A Regional Approach: Mine and UXO Risk Reduction in Vietnam, Laos and Cambodia." *Journal of Mine Action* 9, no. 2 (2006).

What is Agent Orange?" *The Aspen Institute.* Accessed July 7, 2016. https://www.aspeninstitute.org/programs/agent-orange-in-vietnam-program/what-is-agent-orange.

"What is Reparation?" REDRESS. Accessed February 17, 2017. www.redress.org/what-is-reparation/what-is-reparation.

Wilson, Ross. *The Language of the Past.* New York: Bloomsbury Publishing Place, 2016.

Woodward, Angela. "The 1925 Geneva Protocol Goes Digital." *VERTIC Blog.* May 17, 2012. Accessed January 17, 2017. http://www.vertic.org/pages/posts/the-1925-geneva-protocol-goes-digital-298.php.

About the Author

Human rights scholar and activist Ariel S. Garfinkel has a background in international law and women's rights, with a focus on strengthening the enforcement of UN treaty law.

Photo credit: Fletcher Manley

She works with Just Associates (JASS), an international non-profit that partners with global grassroots groups using popular education to amplify women's voices and political influence in promoting the compliance of governments with human rights obligations. Garfinkel also is an officer of Chances for Children International (CCI), a non-profit that enables grassroots organizations in developing countries to ensure that children have access to an education.

Garfinkel previously worked with Girls Incorporated teaching women's rights and financial literacy, as well as with AmeriCorps on food security for new immigrant families.

She holds an M.A. in Human Rights from Columbia University, magna cum laude, and a B.A. from Mount Holyoke College. A Massachusetts native, Garfinkel has lived and worked in Guatemala, Spain, Uganda, and Oman. She currently resides in Washington, D.C.

She can be reached at scofflawbook@gmail.com.